It's A
Young World
After All

It's A Young World After All

Exciting Evidences for Recent Creation

Paul D. Ackerman

BAKER BOOK HOUSE
Grand Rapids, Michigan 49506

Sue Paar, illustrator

Copyright 1986 by Paul D. Ackerman

ISBN: 0-8010-0204-4

Seventh printing, November 1991

Library of Congress Catalog Card Number: 86-70157

Printed in the United States of America

To Harold Slusher
for his pioneering work and leadership
in the scientific investigation of evidences
for recent creation

Contents

Acknowledgments

I am grateful to the following friends for their help in the preparation of this book. In the area of general editing, the suggestions of Sue Paar, Allen Hall, and Ed Hauser were greatly appreciated. On technical matters, the inputs of Bob Gentet, Ken Ham, Harold Slusher, and Carl Wieland were essential. Finally, I wish to express gratitude to my dear friend Ellen Myers, whose support, encouragement, prayers, and fellowship over the years have borne fruit not only in this book but in many other areas of my Christian walk. God bless you all.

Introduction

Am I a God at hand, saith the LORD, *and not a God afar off?*
                                                    Jer. 23:23

The challenge that creation scientists have raised against Darwinian evolution has been carried forward with increasing success in every quarter. In debates on college campuses in the United States and other Western nations, such heroes of the movement as Henry Morris and Duane Gish have carried the battle into bastions of the educational and scientific establishment where Darwinism in its modern form has had dominance for many decades. These debates have been a triumph for the cause of creationism and an embarrassment for evolutionists. As Robert F. Smith, a member of the Western Missouri Affiliate of the American Civil Liberties Union, put it:

> For the past five years, I have closely followed creationist literature and have attended lectures and debates on related issues. . . . Based solely on the scientific arguments pro and con, I have been forced to conclude that scientific creationism is not only a viable theory, but that it has achieved parity with (if not superiority over) the normative theory of biological evolution. That this should now be the case is somewhat surprising, particularly in view of what most of us were taught in primary and secondary school.

In practical terms, the past decade of intense activity by scientific creationists has left most evolutionist professors unwilling to debate the creationist professors. Too many of the evolutionists have been publicly humiliated in such debates by their own lack of erudition and by the weaknesses of their theory.[1]

In Perspective

At this point the war centering around Darwinism and its control over the scientific discussion of origins is going well for the creationists, and evolution is being defeated in many battles. But there is one issue that has yet to receive its proper due. I am speaking of the issue of "age." Even for many creation scientists and Christian laymen, the issue has been considered one to be avoided. Many Christians have been fearful of taking the initiative on this subject. They feel that since evolution has too strong a case for long age periods, creationism can only suffer and be embarrassed by bringing up the topic.

There is a roughly parallel view held by the evolutionists. They feel that to have challenged Darwin was an act both arrogant and ignorant, but to question the millions and billions of years of time—supposedly extending back beyond the reach of man's historical experience—can only be characterized as insane. To the average person it is certainly more bizarre and mind boggling to question modern scientific conclusions regarding the age of things than it is to debate the general question of evolution. Thus, the matter has often been treated by even some of the most stalwart defenders of creationism as a skeleton in the closet. The purpose of this book is to open the closet door.

Of all the topics that constitute the arsenal of the scientific

1. Robert F. Smith, "Origins and Civil Liberties," *Creation Social Science and Humanities Quarterly,* 3 (Winter 1980): 23–24.

creationists and their challenge to the dominance of the evolutionist establishment, there is none stronger than the case for a recent creation. Yet many fellow Christians, who have finally been persuaded by and have become generally sympathetic to the great body of anti-evolution arguments and evidences, are still afraid of the age issue. They are dead wrong in this fearfulness. The fact is that the age issue is one of the creationist's strongest areas. Yet it remains the least understood.

The case for a young universe stands at the same place where the battle against Darwinian evolution stood just a few years ago, when the majority thought the anti-evolutionists were crazy. As one of my colleagues put it upon first hearing that I was a creationist, "Not believing in evolution is like not believing in gravity." Today, just a short time later, the whole situation has been turned around so that Darwinism is on the defensive. The same thing can and must happen on the question of age. As Caleb reported back to Moses after spying out the land of Canaan, "Let us go up at once, and possess it; for we are well able to overcome it" (Num. 13:30).

Let me be blunt on this matter. Evolutionists around the world have had to learn the hard way that evolution cannot stand up against creationism in any fair and impartial debate situation where the stakes are the hearts and minds of intelligent, undecided—but nevertheless objective and open-minded—audiences. Experience will prove that the same is true for the age issue as well. Evolutionist beliefs regarding the origin and development of life cannot withstand the scrutiny of an informed opposition, and neither can evolutionist claims to the effect that the universe has existed for 10 to 20 billion years and the earth for 4.5 billion years. To delay the collapse of widespread public acceptance of such claims, it will be necessary for evolutionist scientists carefully to avoid debate.

Another Perspective

I first became a "scientific creationist" as a result of evidence and arguments relating to the age issue, and that conversion was one of utter joy. The fact that I came into creationism via the route of joy has always flavored my approach to the subject as I have gone around speaking to church and school audiences. My approach has not been that of one who is bringing a moral mandate for action but rather that of a bearer of extremely good news. "Look!" I want to cry out. "God is alive, the Bible is his word, and the evidence is falling into line around these two great truths. God is doing a mighty work in our midst; let us rejoice and open our eyes of faith." I can only hope that this message of joy will come through to the reader, even as it earlier did to me upon reading my first "creation evidences" book. May God bless you.

1

Moon Dust and the Question of Time

> *. . . Blessed of the Lord be his land . . . for the precious*
> *fruits brought forth by the sun, and for the precious things*
> *put forth by the moon.*   Deut. 33:13—14

The most famous argument that creationists have raised for a
recent creation has to do with the amount of dust on the
moon's surface—the so-called moon-dust evidence. It is also
the age argument that has been most sharply challenged by
evolutionists.[1] Although the status of the evidence related to
this argument is currently in dispute, it is nevertheless a
good place to start, since the logic behind it is easy to
understand and communicate. Many of the arguments get
very technical and are hard both to explain and understand.
A grasp of the moon-dust argument will not only provide
the basis for a suspicion that things may not be so old after
all, but will also prepare the reader to more readily understand the more technical evidences and arguments to follow.
In a historical sense the moon-dust argument is important
because it opened up the issue of the time of creation for
many Bible-believing scientists and scholars. Many were
persuaded to take a new look at possible scientific evidences
for recent creation on the basis of this argument.

The Argument: An Analogy

Suppose a friend comes to visit your house and, while he
thinks you are not looking, pulls his finger across the top of

1. The anti-creationist magazine *Creation/Evolution* has recently published two
articles in rebuttal of the creationists' moon-dust argument: "Space Dust, the Moon's
Surface, and the Age of the Cosmos" by Frank T. Awbrey (Issue XIII, p. 21—29) and
"Footprints in the Dust: The Lunar Surface and Creationism" by Steven N. Shore
(Issue XIV, p. 32–35). (*Creation/Evolution* may be obained from P. O. Box 146,
Amherst Branch, Buffalo, NY 14226-0146.) Creationist astronomer Harold S. Slusher
is currently working on a monograph in rebuttal to the evolutionists' challenges to the
moon-dust argument for a recent creation.

your coffee table and looks at it suspiciously. What is he doing? He is trying to find out how long it has been since the coffee table was dusted. He is treating the accumulated dust on the table as a kind of clock, a device that measures the time that passes between dustings. If the time since the last dusting has been short, there should be very little buildup of dust or none at all. If, on the other hand, you are not much of a housekeeper, and it has been a long time since your last dusting, then the amount of dust on the coffee table will be considerable. The method is all very simple and logical, and it can provide a very good clock for measuring the time since the last dusting. What if your friend finds an eighth of an inch of dust on your table? What if he finds a whole inch of dust? What if there is a foot of dust on your table?

The accumulation of dust on your coffee table serves as a pretty good clock, but there are some important limitations that need to be considered. These limitations have to do with what scientists call "assumptions," or conditions that must be known to read our dust clock properly, but which cannot be observed or tested. The dust on the table is an accurate clock only if these assumptions are actually true. There are three assumptions needed to make our dust clock valid—and, in fact, to make all scientific clocks work. First, the starting conditions must be assumed (How much dust is on the table right after dusting?). Second, the rate of change from the beginning until now must be assumed (How fast is dust building up on the coffee table, and has this rate of accumulation been constant over time?). And third, it must be assumed that the clock has been free of outside tampering over the time span in question (Has someone sneaked into the house and removed some of the dust in some other way?).

One can easily see the importance of these assumptions. Suppose a person is an odd sort who actually likes dust on the coffee table. Every few days the old dust may be carefully wiped away and a fresh batch carefully laid down. Somewhat more realistically, a person might be doing some remodeling work in the basement that resulted in the production of an excessive amount of dust. The point is simple. A clock is only as good as the assumptions behind it.

The Moon and Cosmic Dust

If a clock is only as good as the assumptions behind it, let us try to make some reasonable assumptions about the moon. Scientists know that outer space contains an abundance of tiny specks of material known as cosmic dust. This cosmic dust is constantly falling into our atmosphere, collecting on the earth's surface and mixing with all sorts of other material by the action of wind and water. Such cosmic dust will, in fact, collect on all sizable space bodies such as the moon and planets.

On the basis of various methods such as high-altitude balloons and rockets, scientists over the years have attempted to estimate the amount of cosmic dust in the vicinity of the earth and moon and thus the amount that is currently falling onto the moon's surface. If it is assumed that "in the beginning" the moon's surface was clean of any cosmic dust, that the cosmic dust has been settling on its surface at today's rate ever since, and that no unknown factor has interfered with the accumulating dust in the meantime, one has the basis for a simple clock for estimating the age of the moon and, by implication, the earth and the rest of the solar system.

Long before man ever set foot on the moon, some scientists had argued that there did not appear to be enough cosmic dust in the surface layers of the earth to account for the supposed billions of years of earth's history. However, proponents of "long ages" argued that extensive wind and water erosion had masked the assumed presence. It was felt that the missing cosmic dust would turn up somewhere, perhaps in the deep sediment layers of the oceans. So far it has not.

A Trip to the Moon

In the mid-1960s man was approaching the attainment of an age-old dream, to make a space voyage to the moon. As the long-awaited time drew near, intense excitement (as well as apprehension) grew about what might be found there. Among the most frightening aspects was our old friend— cosmic dust. Although the earth is a living planet with constant wind and water action to mix and erode surface materials, the moon is dead and sterile. As the dust from space slowly filters down onto the moon's surface, there is no erosion to wash or blow it away, so it just sits there collecting deeper and deeper. Since the scientists were convinced that the moon was at least 4.5 billion years old, this prospect of a slow but steady "snow" of space dust over that span of time gave them justifiable cause for alarm.

On the basis of certain measurements, it seemed possible that there might be anywhere from 50 to 180 feet of loosely packed cosmic dust on the moon's surface. The threat was that our manned Lunar Lander would sink down into this loose layer and never be able to blast off for the return trip to earth. Of course, all the prospects were not so grim in nature. We also wanted the first astronauts to plant the American flag on the moon. This was expected to be no problem, since it could be easily tapped down into the cosmic dust layer.

As the time of the first manned landing approached, much concern and controversy over the moon-dust problem remained. In a recent television interview, Bob Hope asked Neil Armstrong what was his greatest fear when he set that first historic foot on the moon's surface. Without hesitation Armstrong responded that his greatest fear was the moon-dust layer that scientists had told the astronauts to expect. Many precautions had been taken. Additional expensive impact probes had been sent to check for safe landing sites, and, most important of all, one

Astronaut Aldrin walks near the "duck foot" footpad of the Lunar Lander Eagle
NASA photo

very crucial addition to the landing vehicle was made. Huge duck-feet landing pods were attached to the legs of the Lunar Lander so that it would safely settle down without sinking into the theorized dust layer.

The great day came. The space vehicle roared into orbit and then out into the void. Across thousands of miles of distance it flew, finally taking position in orbit around the moon. The lander detached and, as all of earth watched, the Eagle slowly descended. July 20, 1969. *Mare Tranquillitatis.* "One small step for a man, one giant leap for mankind," said Neil Armstrong.

Testimony of the Dust

A great witness spanned out across the heavens that day as Neil Armstrong stood on the moon and tried to plant the American flag by hammering it down into the supposed billions of years of accumulated cosmic dust. Neil Armstrong hammered, but the flag would not budge, because the anticipated dust layer was simply not there. Oh, of course, it was there, but if the calculations indicating the rate of dust accumulation were accurate, there was not a billion years' worth of dust, nor was there a million years' worth of dust. There was, in fact, only a few thousand years' worth of dust on the moon's surface.

The cosmic-dust evidence revealed an intriguing possibility. Was this issue of how old things are not settled after all? Perhaps the creation was younger than some proposed. Creationists began to take another look at the evidence relating to this age issue, and what they have discovered is simply astounding. It begins to appear that the creation is not vastly ancient, as we have been taught from earliest school days. In fact, it may be quite young.

Evolutionists' Counter-Arguments

Most evolutionists do not accept the conclusions of creationists regarding the moon-dust clock or any of the other clocks presented in this book. Some do, of course, but then they are no longer evolutionists, because the evolutionary scheme requires great lengths of time. An evolutionist *must* hypothesize vast eons for the process of evolution to work. Therefore, some other explanation of the small amount of dust needs to be found.

Old Evidence

The most frequent counter-argument to the creationists' moon-dust evidence has been the suggestion that prior to the Apollo moon mission the overwhelming majority of scientists did not believe there would be much dust and that only a minority fringe group thought otherwise. The evidence indicates that this is not the case, and estimates are that as much as an extra one billion dollars was spent prior to the first Apollo moon mission because of concern about the dust problem. *The Rand McNally New Concise Atlas of the Universe* states, "The theory that the Maria were covered with deep layers of soft dust was current until well into the 1960s."[2] As mentioned earlier, Neil Armstrong, the first man on the moon, confirmed on national television that this was his biggest concern at the time of his first moon walk.

The best source of documentation that evolutionists did believe in the deep dust layer is found in textbooks written prior to the rise of the creation-science movement. Evolutionists were much more candid when they did not know that there was significant opposition to the evolutionist world view. Thus, in 1971, astronomer Robert T. Dixon wrote in his textbook *Dynamic Astronomy,* "The moon was for many years characterized as having a thick layer of dust covering its surface, into which an object would sink if it landed on the moon."[3]

The most concrete evidence that there was genuine belief in the expected deep moon-dust layer is the fact of the modifications to the Lunar Lander. The duck feet that were added are an obvious witness to the serious apprehension concerning the calculations and measurements that led to the prediction of a deep moon-dust layer.

2. *The Rand McNally New Concise Atlas of the Universe* (London: Mitchell Beazley Pub. Ltd. [87–89 Shaftesbury Ave., London W1V 7AD], 1978), p. 41.

3. Robert T. Dixon, *Dynamic Astronomy* (Englewood Cliffs, NJ: Prentice Hall, Inc., 1971), p. 149.

New Evidence

In recent years a more serious challenge to the creationists' claims regarding the moon dust has been raised by the evolutionists.[4] Some of the data collected by orbiting satellites seem to indicate that the amount of cosmic dust in the vicinity of the earth and moon may be much less than earlier measurements indicated. If this is the case, it is argued that the small amount of dust on the moon's surface creates no problem for the view that it is billions of years old.

Harold S. Slusher, the creationist astronomer who has been most closely involved with this issue, has recently been involved in an intensive review of NASA data on the matter and is finding that the higher estimates of the amount of cosmic dust filtering onto the earth and moon are clearly vindicated by the evidence. For example, he reports in recent private correspondence that radar, rocket, and satellite data published in 1976 by NASA and the Smithsonian Institution show that a tremendous amount of cosmic dust is present in the space around the earth and moon.[5] In addition, the evolutionist conception of the solar system's origin assumes much more dust in the past than is currently present. Finally, there are many factors known to remove this dust as time passes (see chapter 3). Therefore, the weight of the evidence is clearly in favor of a recent creation. The moon-dust evidence is a very powerful witness that the solar system is much younger than most evolutionists believe.

---

4. See footnote 1.

5. G. S. Hawkings, ed., *Meteor Orbits and Dust, Smithsonian Contributions to Astrophysics,* vol. 2 (Washington, D.C.: Smithsonian Institution and NASA, 1976).

2

"Fossil" Meteorites

*For God is my King of old, working salvation in the
midst of the earth.*   *Ps. 74:12*

There is another impressive timepiece that works on exactly
the same principle as the cosmic-dust clock and thus provides
an important verification of a recent creation. This clock
deals not with tiny cosmic-dust particles but with larger
chunks of space material known as meteors. A meteor is a
chunk of rock that travels through space until it happens to
fall into the path of the earth. When the meteor approaches
the earth it makes contact with the atmosphere, and the
resulting friction with atmospheric gas causes the meteoritic
rock to heat up. As it heats up more and more, it begins to
glow and finally burns with intense heat and light.

On a clear night these meteors are often visible as they
streak across the sky. Most often such meteors are fairly small
and completely burn up and disintegrate in the atmosphere
before reaching the ground. However, some of them are able
to survive long enough to reach the earth's surface, where
they impact with tremendous force. Such bodies are then
called meteorites, and they are recognizable not so much by
their appearance but most importantly by their high nickel
content. How do these meteorites form a clock?

A Rain Gauge

Consider a rain gauge and how it works. We have a
container that is open at the top. When it rains a certain
number of raindrops will just happen to hit the opening, and
the water from these drops will collect in the container. We
can then go out after it has stopped raining and tell how
much it rained by measuring the amount of water in the
container.

Although we would seldom want to do so, it is possible

with a slight modification in procedure to turn the rain gauge into a kind of clock. Let us assume that we live in a location where it rains continuously and at a known rate. When we set a container outside under these circumstances we have a kind of clock, because we can assume that the more water in the container, the *longer* the container has been outside exposed to the steady shower of rain. If there is very little water, we know the container has not been out or opened for very long. If, on the other hand, there is much water, we know the container has been exposed to the rain for quite a while. Now, back to the matter of meteorites.

The Geologic Column as a Meteor-Shower Gauge

According to the theory of evolution and its requirement of eons of time for earth history, the "geologic column" has been gradually building up for hundreds of millions of years. The geologic column is the name geologists give to the layers of sedimentary rock we can see, for example, when a hill is cut away to make a roadbed for a highway. One of the most spectacular views of such stratified layers is provided by the Grand Canyon. Evolutionists believe that these rock layers have been building up gradually for millions of years.

If these millions of years were a reality there would have been countless numbers of meteors encountering the earth's atmosphere. As previously mentioned, the vast majority of these meteors would have burned up before reaching the ground, but a small percentage would reach the earth's surface each year as meteorites. With the passage of vast amounts of evolutionary time, these accumulating meteorites would be incorporated into the geologic column, and there should be many of them contained in the rock layers today. Paleontologists and other scientists doing research in the geologic rock layers should frequently encounter meteorites.

Most creationist scientists, however, do not believe that

the geologic column has been building up, and thus been open to meteors, for millions of years. They argue, on the basis of a great deal of data and evidence, that the geologic column was laid down quickly under catastrophic conditions and thus has not been exposed to meteorites for very long. If this is the case, there would be very few meteorites in the geologic column and finding one would be a rare occurrence.

On the basis of the opposing recent-creation and evolution models, we have two distinctly different predictions about the number of meteorites in the geologic column. The evolution model predicts a high number of meteorites, which should turn up fairly often in geological research. Recent-creationists, by contrast, expect a very small number of meteorites in the geologic column. Thus, finding one should be an extremely rare event.

What do the data show? A clear result in favor of a recent creation. One survey of the literature a few years ago failed to turn up a single case of a meteorite being found in the geologic column.[1] The meteorite clock reads clearly to the effect that the earth is not very old.[2]

---

1. P. Stevenson, "Meteoritic Evidence for a Young Earth," *Creation Research Society Quarterly* 12 (June 1975): 23; cited in R. L. Wysong, *The Creation-Evolution Controversy* (Midland, MI: Inquiry Press, 1976): 171.

2. In the introduction of this book I mentioned the joy with which I became a scientific creationist. I stumbled across a little book by Henry Morris called *The Remarkable Birth of Planet Earth*. It seemed like an intriguing topic so I bought it. What I expected to find was an array of dogmatic assertions and appeals to blind acceptance of authority. Instead, what I found was a tightly argued case for biblical creation, much of it having to do with the age of things. In terms of my background and training in scientific method and logic, this was the kind of reasoning and use of evidence one could applaud and emulate.

Once reading began, I found I could not put the book down. It was fascinating. At the end, Morris listed a number of evidences indicating that the earth is young. Reading down the list, I reached a particular item that for me was the "straw that broke the camel's back." That evidence, which was and still is very special to me, is none other than the "fossil" meteorite data presented in this chapter. Jumping from my chair, I began to dance through the house with joy. My wife, as she often did in those early days of my life as a Christian, thought that I had gone crazy. Happily, she has now joined me in this "craziness."

3

The Solar Janitor

*To him that made great lights . . . The sun to rule by day.
. . . The moon and stars to rule by night: for his mercy
endureth for ever.*   Ps. 136:7–9

Once scientists have an eye for them, the world around us
reveals an abundance of clocks. Furthermore, as time goes by
and we learn more about how to read the clocks of nature
properly, their testimony is increasingly clear that things are
not so old after all. The evidence of the moon-dust and
meteorite clocks are only two of a host of witnesses for a
recent creation.

In the past, when almost all scientists believed that evolution was true, they had no choice on the age issue. A
dedicated evolutionist cannot be open-minded on this question, because evolution absolutely requires vast amounts of
time. Thus, for evolutionist scientists the question has never
really been "How old is the universe?" but rather "*How* is the
universe old?" Since they "knew" it was old, clocks had to be
found and interpreted according to this "known" antiquity.

But, as we have learned more and more, the testimony of
the clocks has grown more insistent that there is something
drastically wrong with the evolutionist scenario and its
claims of an ancient cosmos. It used to be put forth as a charge
against the simple faith of believers in the straightforward
record of creation found in the Bible that the account could
not really be "God's Word" because that would mean God
was a deceiver. If God has created all things out of nothing
only a few thousand years ago, he could not then proceed to
fill the universe with clear "evidences" that the universe was
old and that vast ages inhabited by strange creatures had
preceded man's entry into the world. Now the tables have
turned, and the believer can throw the challenge back by
saying, "If the universe was created as long ago as the
evolutionists claim, why does it look so young? God is surely
not a deceiver."

Solar Cleanup Clock

If one stops to think about it, a person engaged in a cleanup job presents us with another kind of clock. For instance, in sweeping the carpet, the amount of carpet that has been swept makes for a kind of clock that indicates how long the janitor has been working at the job. The more carpet that has been swept, the more time has passed since the job was started. In this regard it turns out that the sun in a certain sense resembles a janitor within the solar system, constantly working away to "sweep" and "sort" some of its smaller particles.

The Poynting-Robertson Effect

A good part of this janitorial work occurs by what scientists call the Poynting-Robertson effect after the scientists who discovered and explained it.[1] This is one of the most intriguing solar janitorial clocks indicating a recent creation. It has an imposing name that sounds impressive, but the idea is fairly easy to understand.

An Analogy

I will use a simple illustration to explain. Assume that a steady rain shower is occurring and that there is no wind. If you sit in your car, the drops appear to come straight down from the sky. In fact, they do come straight down since there is no wind. However, if you start to drive the car, the drops of rain begin to appear

1. Much of the material for this chapter was obtained from Harold S. Slusher, *Age of the Cosmos: ICR Technical Monograph #9* (San Diego: Institute for Creation Research [2716 Madison Ave., San Diego, CA 92116], 1980).

as if they are coming down at an angle directly into your front windshield; the faster you drive, the shallower the angle becomes.

The same thing holds true if you are standing in the rain with an umbrella. If there is no wind, the drops come straight down and you hold the umbrella directly over your head. However, as you begin to walk you have to tip your umbrella forward in order to keep dry. The faster you walk, the more you tip the umbrella. The crucial point in understanding the Poynting-Robertson effect is that even though the raindrops are coming straight down, they strike an object *at an angle* as it moves through the rain.

Now, although we don't think much about it, a raindrop has weight and substance. It hits your car's windshield with a certain force as you drive along. The force that the rain exerts pushes against the forward movement of the car since the raindrops are coming in at an angle caused by your car's movement. They beat against the front of the car and tend to slow it down. If we could get fine enough measurements, we would find that your car has to burn just a little more gas when driving through the rain, because it takes just a little more power to push the car along the road against the force of the raindrops.

Back to Outer Space

The above illustration provides all the basic components for understanding the Poynting-Robertson effect in space. The counterpart of the rain is the light radiation emitted by the sun, and the counterpart of your car is any object moving through space in orbit around the sun or some other body in the solar system. Light radiation from the sun may be viewed as little particles called photons. These photons move on a straight line out from the sun in all directions. As an object in space moves along its orbit, it encounters these photons of light, just as one's car encounters raindrops in a storm. Furthermore, these photons exert a certain force to impede the forward movement of the object, and over time the object will lose speed. As it loses speed, its orbit is changed so that it falls closer and closer to the sun. Eventually the object will be slowed down to the point where it can no longer stay in orbit, and the sun's gravitational force will pull it in. In this way, as well as others, the sun is constantly working as a janitor and sweeping the solar system clean of debris.

The Poynting-Robertson Clock

It turns out that the slowing effect of Poynting-Robertson is directly related to the mass of the object being considered. Just as raindrops might be more of a factor in slowing an automobile than a large truck, so it is that smaller objects in space are affected more than larger ones. Considering only the Poynting-Robertson effect, scientists can calculate how long it would take for objects of a particular mass and orbital distance from the sun to be "swept up." As it turns out, the calculations show that small particles such as the cosmic dust sphericals we discussed in chapter 1 should be swept up in a relatively short time. The fact that they exist in abundance in outer space, as determined by a number of lines of observational evidence, is a strong indication that the solar system is not nearly as old as evolutionist scientists maintain.

More important than the small-particle considerations, however, are the results of careful measurements made by the famous astronomer Fred Whipple at Harvard University. Whipple realized that over time the Poynting-Robertson effect would sort out and disperse meteor streams in accordance with the mass of individual objects making up the stream.

Scientists do not know where meteor streams originate. Many streams are thought to be formed by the debris left over from the breakup of comets as they come too close to the sun and are pulled apart. Other streams are thought to be left over from the formation of the solar system. Some believe that meteoritic material originated about three billion years ago when something happened between the orbits of Mars and Jupiter. Perhaps some previously existing planet broke up or perhaps there was some collision involving the asteroid belt. No one is sure about the origin of the streams, but it has frequently been claimed that they are quite old.

When the earth passes through one of these meteor streams, it produces the popular spectacle of a meteor shower. Of relevance to the issue of time and Poynting-Robertson is that individual chunks of material in a meteor stream vary greatly in mass. Some chunks are small, some large, and some in between. Whipple calculated that over time the various pieces of material in a given stream would be sorted out according to size by the Poynting-Robertson effect. Initially all sizes of debris would be jumbled together in the stream. But, as time went by, the smaller objects would be pulled more quickly toward the sun, with the larger objects lagging behind. After a while the meteor stream would be nicely and neatly sorted. Furthermore, the degree of the sorting and the amount of separation between objects of different sizes would provide a clock for measuring the age of the meteor stream.

Using careful photographic techniques to examine meteors burning up in the earth's atmosphere during a number of meteor showers, Whipple and his research team found *no dispersion whatsoever* in any of the meteor streams studied. Whipple concluded that the meteor streams studied must be quite recent in their origin. As creationist astronomer Harold Slusher writes regarding this finding:

> If there is not this dispersion, this spreading out of material into smaller and smaller orbits, how can meteor streams be more than 10,000 years old? Meteor showers do not show the dispersion effect that the Poynting-Robertson effect predicts; therefore, they cannot be old.[2]

2. Harold S. Slusher, "A Young Universe," *Bible-Science Newsletter* 13 (January 1975): 1ff.

Implications

The sweeping action of the Poynting-Robertson effect and other processes such as one termed "sputtering" are extremely important in this question of the age of things. "Sputtering" is the name given to the effect of collisions of photons with small particles in space. The collisions break off small bits of matter and thus in time destroy the small particles. In terms of its sweeping effect, sputtering is much more rapid than Poynting-Robertson in clearing the solar system of small particles. Furthermore, what is true of our sun is true of the stars as well. Just as the sun is surrounded by an abundance of dust material that should have been swept clean long ago *if* the solar system were as old as generally claimed by evolutionists, so are many stars surrounded by huge clouds of dust and gas. In some cases these stars are radiating energy 100,000 times faster than our sun, thus speeding up the sweeping action by a commensurate amount. How can these stars be "old" and still be surrounded by so much material? The creationist answer is simply that they are not old; the evidence clearly indicates they cannot be.

Short-Period Comets

One of the themes we want to emphasize repeatedly in this book is that if evolution is true, the earth and the rest of the solar system and cosmos must be extremely old. The problem with this for evolutionist scientists is that since—as the creationists maintain—the overwhelming weight of actual physical evidence indicates that things are quite young, the evolutionists must come up with fantastic and totally implausible mechanisms to explain how things are kept going for the billions of years evolution requires. An excellent example of

Comet West © Royer and Padilla.

this is the amazing idea that volcanoes on giant planets occasionally belch out new comets into orbit around the sun.[3] We shall return to this idea after we first consider the issue of short-period comets.

Short-period comets constitute one of the most easily understood examples of our so-called solar-janitor effect. Comets are very strange objects that orbit around the sun. Although it is not usually realized, the glowing, visible shroud of gas surrounding many comets is larger in terms of volume than even the planet Jupiter, and in a few instances it is greater than the sun itself. The inner core, or comet proper, however, is quite small and invisible to observation from the earth. Scientists do not yet know what the core is made of, but current evidence has led most to characterize it as a "very dirty iceberg."

When we think of comets, we naturally picture the long visible trail, but the fact is that through most of each orbital

3. Slusher, *Age of the Cosmos,* p. 48.

period no trail is visible. It is only when a comet approaches close to the sun that the famous trail appears. This trail is comprised of material that is in effect being burned off the body of the comet; every time it passes close to the sun more of its substance is burned off and forever lost. This loss of material with each sun passage is the basis for a very important clock. The solar janitor is not only sweeping the solar system clean of tiny bits of material via sputtering and the Poynting-Robertson effect; it is also cleaning the solar system of comets by burning off a substantial portion of their mass during each close approach to the sun.

Over the centuries the destruction of many short-period comets has been observed and recorded. Sometimes they break up into smaller pieces, and sometimes they disappear entirely during their close approach to the sun. There have been ten recorded observations of comet destruction in this century. The perplexing problem of all this for evolutionists is that the average life span for these short-period comets is on the order of only 1,500 to 10,000 years. This means that if the solar system were even as old as one-half million years, there should be no short-period comets left. Yet there is an abundance of them.

Looking for Solutions

Evolutionists are well aware of the situation described here with regard to the life span of short-period comets. The only obvious solution to the dilemma is to find a source of supply so that the population of short-period comets can be continually replenished. As previously mentioned, it is in this search for solutions that evolutionist scientists sometimes drift off into the realm of the fantastic and the impossible. Evolutionists have proposed three suggestions regarding how the solar system might be resupplied with short-period comets.

Jupiter and Long-Period Comets

The first suggestion is that short-period comets are captured gravitationally by Jupiter from the large number of
long-period comets, which have orbits that take them so far
from the sun that they would pass into the interior regions of
the solar system only once in perhaps a million years. The
gravitational-attraction conjecture is that occasionally a long-
term comet passes close to Jupiter and in the process its orbit
is drastically changed so that it becomes a new short-period
comet.

Several difficulties have led to the general rejection of this
surmise. For one thing there are simply not enough near
passes between long-period comets and Jupiter to account for
the number of short-period comets in existence. For another,
the orbits of the short-period comets rule out this possibility.

In the long term of the evolutionist time scale there is also
a problem with the supply of long-period comets. The most
popular suggested source of long-period comets is referred to
as "Ort's cloud" after astronomer J. H. Ort, who guessed
that there might be a huge spherical shell of comets surrounding our solar system at about one-fifth of the distance
to the nearest star. He conjectured that the gravitational
disturbance caused by occasional passing stars or planets
might alter the orbits of some of the comets in such a way as
to send them into the interior of the solar system as new
long-term comets. Suffice it to say that there is no direct
observational evidence of either the shell (Ort's cloud) or
prospective stars or planets to disturb it. Calculations of the
orbits of existing long-period comets also present difficulties
for the theory. Finally, how such a cloud of comets itself
might evolve is a very serious problem for evolutionists.

The Asteroid Belt

A second popular idea among evolutionists is that perhaps short-period comets originate in the asteroid belt. It has been suggested that a close encounter between an asteroid and one of the giant planets might result in a breakup of the asteroid and the creation of one or more short-period comets. A number of difficulties lead to rejection of this idea. As was the case under the surmise of their being captured by Jupiter, the orbits of the short-period comets will not fit into the asteroid-origin scheme. More important, the physical make-up of asteroids and comets is totally different.

Volcanoes in Space

A third speculation about short-period comets seems more like science fiction than reasonable scientific conjecture. This idea suggests that comets are belched out by erupting volcanoes, most probably on Jupiter. Numerous critics have pointed out that the problems with this notion are monumental. Foremost among the difficulties is that the idea has no observational or theoretical foundation whatsoever. There is no known planetary mechanism to impart the force needed to expel a comet into orbit. The physical makeup of comets does not fit the idea of such an origin; the orbits of short-period comets do not bear the necessary relationship to Jupiter or any other giant planet to be accounted for by the volcanic-eruption notion; and, most critically, if a chunk of material were expelled upward from the surface of Jupiter or some other giant planet with the estimated 370-miles-per-second speed required to put it into orbit around the sun, it would burn up and vaporize in the atmosphere. To quote astronomer Harold Slusher from his book *Age of the Cosmos*:

... we know that even in earth's much shallower atmosphere meteors ... are completely vaporized. This alone should make it clear that there is no possibility of anything remotely resembling a comet coming out of a planet. The requisite high speed would cause it to vaporize at once.[4]

Conclusion

In concluding this matter of the apparent recent origin of short-period comets, astronomer Harold Slusher has stated:

The failure to find a mechanism to resupply comets or to form new comets would seem to lead to the conclusion that the age of the comets and hence the solar system is quite young, on the order of just several thousand years at most. ... The obvious is that the solar system has been operating on a short time scale since its creation.[5]

4. Ibid., p. 49.
5. Ibid., pp. 53–54.

4

Of Smoldering Embers

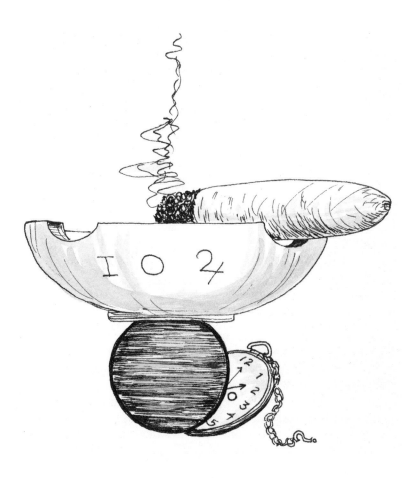

He looketh on the earth, and it trembleth: he toucheth the hills, and they smoke.   Ps. 104:32

Imagine that you are hiking in a remote wilderness area seldom visited by man. You are making your way through winding forest trails to a secluded cabin owned by a friend back in the city. He has volunteered his cabin as a much-needed vacation spot, assuring you that it is locked up securely and has not been occupied since his last visit over a year ago. You arrive at the cabin, unlock the door, and enter. Although the cabin appears totally empty, on the table in front of you is an ashtray containing a lighted cigar, and the fireplace reveals still-smoldering remnants of an earlier fire.

The simplest and most logical assessment of this situation would be to conclude that your friend is quite mistaken about no one living in his cabin. Someone has most certainly been here, and quite recently at that. The prudent course of action would be to be very wary of possible danger from this unknown occupant.

On the other hand, if there is some reason why you are absolutely wedded to belief in the owner's information that the cabin has been vacant for over a year, then you would be forced to figure out how a cigar and fireplace could continue to burn for such a great length of time. There must be something very bizarre about a cigar and firewood that can burn for over a year. Every suggestion you come up with would seem farfetched to any informed person. What is more, closer observations and additional data would only make matters worse.

If you can understand the absurdity of a suggestion that a cigar and fireplace could burn for a year and that a person could figure out realistic mechanisms to make such a thing possible, you can understand something of the dilemmas produced by results from our space research program.

The Moon That Blew Its Top

Do you remember the news coverage of the two Jupiter explorations by our Voyager space probes in 1979? Among the spectacular scenes of the planet and accompanying satellites was a most amazing sight—a volcano erupting on one of the moons of Jupiter, Io, at the very moment one of the Voyager's television cameras was trained on the satellite during the fly-by. Why was this event the cause of such excitement on the part of the NASA scientists? In their view the moons of Jupiter were formed at the same time as the planet itself and are about 4.5 billion years old. Small bodies such as this particular satellite would be expected to lose the interior heat and dynamism that produces volcanic activity relatively quickly and thus would be expected to have long since become cold and inactive. The occurrence of a volcano, however, tells us that the object is still hot and geologically active in its interior. Quoting from a report that appeared in *Life* magazine following the Voyager mission:

> The big surprise of the Voyager mission was Io, one of Jupiter's inner moons. Instead of being cold, dead and otherwise moonlike, Io proved to be literally bubbling with volcanoes. Voyager's cameras witnessed one eruption on the moon's rim . . . that spewed fire and brimstone more than 100 miles into space . . . . earth was hitherto considered the only geologically active body in the solar system, but Io was found to be even more violent.[1]

Scientists have puzzled over the problem posed by the geologically active Io and have offered some possible solutions, the most favored of which is some form of gravitational

1. "Eyes on Jupiter," *Life* (May 1979), p. 46.

"pumping" by Jupiter and its other moons. Expert critics, however, have pointed out that this is only a stopgap solution and will really not do the job of explaining Io's geological activity over extended evolutionist time spans.

How can a moon of Jupiter be so old and still so hot and active? How can a cigar burn for a year? The problem is the same, and so is the solution, however unthinkable to evolutionist scientists. Maybe Io, just like the smoldering cigar, is not so old after all.

Of course, depending on specific existing conditions, the knife of discovery can sometimes cut the other way. The opposite difficulty was discovered during the Apollo explorations of our own moon. Lunar material was found to be very high in radioactivity. Scientists conferring on this and other matters at the Fourth Lunar Science Conference wondered how the moon can be very old and not be intensely hot or even melting from the accumulation of heat from the radiation. As Wysong states in his excellent book, *The Creation-Evolution Controversy:* "But the moon is rigid, and some [scientists] argue the moon has a cool interior. This rigidity and relative coolness of the moon [given its high level of radioactivity] speaks for its youth—less than 50,000 years old."[2]

Along these same lines, the lunar soil showed not only an abundance of radioactive material but also types of radiation that simply should not be in existence if the moon was very old. Again quoting from Wysong:

> Short-lived U-236 and Th-230 isotopes found in lunar materials are taken as testimony for youth. If the moon were of great age, the short-lived isotopes would have long since decayed and thus be presently absent. Yet they are not

2. R. L. Wysong, *The Creation-Evolution Controversy* (Midland, MI: Inquiry Press, 1976), p. 177. This book is available from Inquiry Press, 4925 Jefferson, Midland, MI 48640, or from the Bible-Science Association, Inc., 2911 E. 42nd St., Minneapolis, MN 55406. The Bible-Science Association carries a considerable array of creationism resources.

absent, they are in relative abundance. Thus, according to this method, the age of the moon should be spoken of in terms of thousands of years, not millions or billions.[3]

Saturn's Rings

The same situation pertains to our discoveries about the rings of Saturn. Scientists were totally flabbergasted by the appearance of turbulence and instability in these rings. Rings that have stayed in place for 4.5 billion years should be in a very stable condition. Signs of instability and bizarre temporary physical conditions are extremely perplexing and seem to violate known and fully confirmed basic laws of physics. If, on the other hand, the rings are only a few thousand years old, there is no difficulty with known physical laws—just as a cigar that smolders for three or four minutes presents no contradictions to known physical laws.

General Findings of Our Space Program—And a Recent Dramatic Example

The evidence of our space probes indicates that the solar system, despite its reputed great antiquity, is active and alive. For evolutionist scientists the main outcome of our space exploration has been *surprise*. Phrases such as "apparent paradox" and "seems to violate known laws of physics" have abounded. Yet there is nothing in the findings that does not square fully with basic laws of physics, as long as one is willing to give up the idea of vast ages. The data are abundantly clear: the creation is not old; it is young.

An excellent example of what I am talking about occurred in a *Los Angeles Times/Washington Post* wire-service story that

3. Ibid., pp. 177–178.

appeared in a local newspaper in late 1983.[4] The headline
bannered the news—"Dust Rings Our Solar System: NASA
Calls Spacescope Findings 'Spectacular.'" The story reports
the recent scientific discovery that three giant rings of dust
circle the solar system. The discovery of the rings was made
by observational data coming from the Infrared Astronomical
Satellite, an orbiting spacecraft built by the United States,
the Netherlands, and Great Britain. By getting a better view
outside the blanket of earth's atmosphere, the orbiting telescope was able to detect things heretofore invisible to earthbound astronomers.

The project's scientific team leader, Gerry Neugebauer of
the Jet Propulsion Laboratory in California, reports, "This
telescope has been so sensitive that we could see a single
speck of dust with it at a distance of two miles. . . . If you
were to put a baseball into orbit over the East Coast, this
telescope could pick it up on the West Coast."[5] The news
story goes on to relate details of the dust-ring discovery:

> What the telescope picked up that had never been seen
> before were three gigantic dust rings 100 million miles wide
> circling the asteroid belt between Mars and Jupiter 200
> million to 300 million miles from the sun. The dust bands,
> which had never before been seen because they are composed
> of particles too fine to see and too cool to shine, *appear to defy
> the laws of physics* by encircling the asteroid belt in three
> extremely stable and symmetrical rings. "Particles this small
> can only survive in stable orbits for a few ten-thousands of
> years before they are pulled apart by the sun," said Frank Low
> of the University of Arizona. "There must be something that
> replenishes the rings because three stable bands that large
> cannot exist any other way."[6] (Emphasis was added.)

---

4. "Dust Rings Our Solar System," *Wichita Eagle and Beacon*, 10 November 1983,
p. 1A ff.
5. Ibid.
6. Ibid.

The article then continues to report some of the various lines of speculation that evolutionist scientists are engaging in to "keep the cigar burning in the ashtray" for the necessary amount of time.

Conclusion

The evidence in support of a young universe has grown rapidly in recent years as a result of the data explosion stemming from enormous advances in sophisticated technology. Nevertheless, the human factor remains as the most significant component of the equation. In spite of so much evidence to the contrary, the prevailing dogma of evolution maintains its headlock on the scientific community.

Old ideas die hard, and evolution, with its requirement of millions and billions of years of cosmic history is no exception. Millions of tax dollars and untold hours of scientific brainpower are being wasted in an attempt to keep the evolution boat afloat. Harebrained and impossible concepts are being dressed in a cloak of respectability and promoted as serious science. It is time to face the facts: mega-evolution, with its vast prehistoric ages, is dead. The creation is not old; it is young.

5

Pour Me a Rock

He sends forth springs in the valleys; They flow between
the mountains.   *Ps. 104:10,* NASB

Scientists have discovered many wondrous things about the
beautiful world God has created. One of the most surprising
is that the clear and common distinction between solids and
liquids becomes blurred when long periods of time are
involved. We all learned as children that liquids flow and
solids retain their shape, but if enough time is involved,
solids are found to flow just like liquids.

The Concept

Consider trying to make a sculpture out of water. You
would pour it into a mold, where it would assume the
desired shape. As soon as the mold was removed, however,
the water would run down into a puddle on the table. A
sculpture made of honey would last a little longer, but not
much. These facts are well known, since people have a great
deal of experience with these common liquids.

What is not realized is that a sculpture of glass is doing
the same thing as the honey and water but much more
slowly. Given enough time, a glass figurine would also flow
down into a puddle. The flow of glass is exceedingly slow, of
course, but it is fast enough that in the span of a hundred
years the bottom edge of a window pane will measurably and
noticeably thicken.

Granite is one of the hardest and slowest flowing materials
on earth, but even its rate of flow has been measured by
scientists. Long slender bars of granite were cut and hung
horizontally with fixed attachments at both ends. Over a
period of years the long bars bent in the middle as gravity
caused their rock material to flow downward. Flow deforma-

tions of tombstones and other rock monuments can also be observed.

Rock Flow and the Age of the Moon

What does the fact that rock flows have to do with the age of things? An obvious feature of the moon is that in the past it has been battered by numerous collisions with large meteors. These impacts have left the lunar surface heavily scarred. Evolutionists believe that most of these craters were formed early in the moon's history, when the solar system was young and before life was established on earth. The reason for this view is in part that if the moon was bombarded, then from the evolutionist perspective the earth must have been similarly battered. The scars are not apparent on the earth's surface because, unlike the moon, the earth experiences the erosional forces of wind and water which erased the evidence of early violence.

In addition, large-scale bombardment must surely have

Moon craters NASA photo

ceased before life got started or else it would have been wiped out. For example, a current evolutionist conjecture regarding dinosaur extinction is that it resulted from the impact of an asteroid.

Recent-creationists also believe the impact craters were formed early in the moon's existence, but they believe that this was only a few thousand years ago. Thus we have two opposing views about the same phenomenon. Most scientists believe the craters to be at least three billion years old, while a few believe them to be only a few thousand. Is there a way to test and see which view is correct?

Geophysicist and astronomer Harold Slusher of the University of Texas at El Paso, along with Glenn Morton and Richard Mandock, have worked on this problem and discovered a simple and seemingly decisive solution. They have done so by considering the flow rates (viscosity) of the lunar rock material that forms the moon craters.[1] If the moon were covered with water, impact craters would last only a few seconds. If it were made of honey, craters would last just a bit longer. Since the moon is covered with rock, impact craters last a much longer time, but how long depends upon the kind of rock and its viscosity or rate of flow.

The rocks brought back from the moon by our Apollo astronauts have been carefully studied and found to be virtually identical with a kind of earth rock called basalt. The discovery that the moon's surface is made up of basalt-type rock rules out the possibility that lunar craters are more than a few thousand years old! The viscosity or flow-rate value used by scientists is on the order of a hundred million times too low (the higher the value, the slower the flow rate) for the craters to have lasted three or four billion years. Even if the lunar surface were made of granite, the viscosity value of that granite would be ten million times too low to hold the crater shape for three billion years. If the lunar surface were made

1. Material for this chapter is taken from Glenn R. Morton, Harold S. Slusher, and Richard E. Mandock, "The Age of Lunar Craters," *Creation Research Society Quarterly* 20 (September 1983): 105–108.

of the same rock material as the earth's mantle, the viscosity value would be too low by a factor of one hundred thousand.

Conclusion

Thus the physical evidence is loud and clear to the effect that the craters of the moon cannot be as old as evolutionists claim. In fact, the data indicate that the craters must be only a few thousand years old. To quote the research report of Morton, Slusher, and Mandock:

> As can be seen, the lunar craters cannot last longer than a few million years for any reasonable value of the viscosity. If the viscosity of granite is the upper limit for the viscosity of basalt, then lunar craters cannot be more than a few thousand years old. . . .
> The evidence presented here demonstrates that the lunar surface and the craters on it are relatively young structures.[2]

2. Ibid., pp. 106–107.

6

Is the Sun Shrinking?

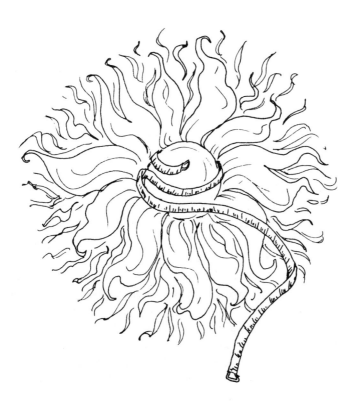

. . . thou hast prepared the light and the sun. Ps. 74:16

What causes the sun to shine? Prior to the rise of Darwin's evolution theory, the great nineteenth-century scientist Hermann von Helmholtz proposed a simple and effective model— gravitational collapse. The only problem with the concept was that it would not allow anything approaching the vast amounts of time demanded by the theory of evolution. If the sun produced its energy by gravitational collapse, the sun could last no longer than a few million years, and for evolution to have even a ghost of a chance much more time is required.

Around the turn of the century, the famous scientist Lord Kelvin created difficulties for evolutionists by presenting a number of powerful arguments against the long ages needed by their theory. In a widely heralded debate with the famous evolutionist Thomas Huxley, Lord Kelvin tore the evolutionists' position to shreds with simple and straightforward physical arguments that the earth and solar system were not old enough for life to have arisen by Darwin's proposed evolutionary process. Among Lord Kelvin's arguments on the age issue was the time factor for the sun's survival based upon Helmholtz's accepted model of gravitational collapse. Lord Kelvin had the theory of evolution on the ropes and had seemingly dealt the knockout blow.

What happened? The discovery of atomic radiation changed the whole picture. Evolutionists suddenly took new courage as the phenomenon of atomic radiation seemed to provide the necessary answer to Kelvin's challenge. With regard to the question of why the sun shines, the gravitational-collapse model became unfashionable, and in the 1930s Hans Bethe introduced the currently accepted view that thermonuclear fusion in the sun's core is the source of its energy.

Flies in the Ointment

Neutrinos

Although the nuclear-fusion theory of solar burning is widely accepted in scientific circles, it has one serious drawback. Unfortunately, a large-scale nuclear-fusion reaction in the sun's interior would give almost no indication of its existence, and so the concept is difficult to verify scientifically. As it turns out, however, there is one very expensive method of verification. Princeton astronomer John Bahcall, along with Raymond Davis of the Brookhaven National Laboratory, wrote a research report on this work in 1976.[1]

To "catch" neutrinos (particles released during certain nuclear reactions) and verify the thermonuclear-fusion theory, a large cavity was dug deep underground in a South Dakota gold mine. The necessary apparatus for detecting neutrinos was then constructed. The importance of this research in terms of providing necessary testing of the widely accepted general theory of evolution cannot be overemphasized. As Bahcall and Davis explain:

> One may well ask, why devote so much effort in trying to understand a backyard problem like the sun's thermonuclear furnace? . . . The theory of solar energy generation is . . . important to the general understanding of stellar evolution. . . .
>
> There is a way to directly and quantitatively test the theory of nuclear energy generation in stars like the sun. Of the particles released by the assumed thermonuclear reactions in the solar interior, only one has the ability to penetrate from the center of the sun to the surface and escape into space: the neutrino. Thus neutrinos offer us a unique possibility of "looking" into the solar interior. . . . the theory of

1. John N. Bahcall and Raymond Davis, Jr., "Solar Neutrinos: A Scientific Puzzle," *Science* 191 (1976): 264–267.

stellar aging by thermonuclear burning is widely used in interpreting many kinds of astronomical information and is a *necessary link in establishing such basic data as the ages of the stars*. . . . Thus an experiment designed to capture neutrinos produced by solar thermonuclear reactions is a crucial one for the theory of stellar evolution. . . . It is for . . . these reasons . . . that so much effort has been devoted to the solar neutrino problem [emphasis added].[2]

From a creationist point of view, the results of the neutrino-capture experiments are very exciting, for they indicate that the thermonuclear-fusion theory of solar radiation may be entirely wrong. The sun is not emitting the necessary neutrinos. In an Associated Press story of March 1980, Kevin McKean discusses the impact of the "case of the missing neutrinos":

The neutrino is a particle emitted during certain nuclear reactions, including several of those believed to power the sun. It travels at or near the speed of light, like an invisible ray, and can penetrate miles of very dense matter without striking anything. Trillions of neutrinos from the sun stream through our bodies every second. Because neutrinos can escape from deep within the sun, scientists realized they might be a good way of checking whether the reactions believed to power the sun are really happening. Chemist Ray Davis Jr., of Brookhaven National Laboratory in Brookhaven, N.Y., led a team that set up a neutrino detector nearly a mile underground at the Homestake Gold Mine in Lead, S.D. In nearly a decade of operation the detector has found only one-third the expected number of neutrinos. . . . "It seems to me that we're not even at first base," Bahcall says. "We have just realized we have a ball game and all we know is somebody is out there throwing fastballs at us and we can't even see them."[3]

2. Ibid., p. 264.
3. "The Sun Is Shrinking," *Wichita Eagle and Beacon,* 23 March 1980, p. 6B.

Again quoting from Bahcall and Davis:

> For the past 15 years we have tried, in collaboration with
> many colleagues in astronomy, chemistry, and physics, to
> understand and test the theory of how the sun produces its
> radiant energy (observed on the earth as sunlight). All of us
> have been surprised by the results: there is a large, unexplained
> disagreement between observation and the supposedly well
> established theory. This discrepancy has led to a crisis in the
> theory of stellar evolution; many authors are openly question-
> ing some of the basic principles and approximations in this
> supposedly dry (and solved) subject.[4]

Evidence from the Stars

Failure to find the predicted neutrinos was the most direct
and telling of a number of serious flies in the ointment of the
thermonuclear-fusion theory of solar burning. In a 1975
article, geo- and astrophysicist Harold Slusher explained two
other difficulties.[5]

First, the chemical composition of stars should change as
they proceed through their supposed thermonuclear life cycle.
However, observational studies of what should be stars of
vastly different ages show them all to have roughly the same
chemical composition. This presents a real enigma for the
evolutionary nuclear-process theory.

Second, and equally damaging, is the frequent occurrence
of star clusters that are gravitationally bound and thus
presumably originating at the same time, yet containing stars
of vastly different ages on the thermonuclear-burn sequence.
Some cluster observations are so mind boggling from an
evolutionist point of view that even if there were not an

---

4. Bahcall and Davis, "Solar Neutrinos," p. 264.
5. Harold S. Slusher, "A Young Universe," *Bible-Science Newsletter* 13 (January 1975): 1ff.

abundance of other empirical evidences, these alone ought to rule out the vast-age concept. The most dramatic is a cluster of four stars in the Trapezium of the Orion nebula. These four stars are moving away from a common point at a high rate of speed. If the motion of these four stars is projected backward at their present speed, their paths lead to a common point of origin only about 10,000 years ago. Yet, according to the accepted scheme, the stars in the cluster are vastly older than 10,000 years. Slusher asks, "If the cluster cannot be old, how can the stars be old?" Indeed, this amazing cluster raises the question of whether the creation itself should be considered as older than 10,000 years.

A Temperature Dilemma

Among the other difficulties discovered prior to the conclusive neutrino results, one of the most important is a paradox between the expected nuclear-fusion temperature history of the sun and the temperature history of the earth, based on fossil evidence. If the sun is producing its energy by nuclear fusion on an evolutionist time scale, then a billion years ago it should have been fainter and cooler than it is now.[6] Although the expected difference in solar energy output would be only 5 percent, that difference is more than enough to cause the earth to be solidly frozen in a crust of ice. The fossil evidence, however, indicates that the early history of the earth was tropical and warmer than it is now. To quote physicists Michael J. Newman of Cal Tech and Robert T. Rood of the University of Virginia, "The discrepancy . . . indicates that there is a serious problem with our understanding of the structure of the sun, or of our understanding of the earth's climate or both."[7]

With the completion of the solar-neutrino research pro-

6. "The Faint Young Sun and the Warm Earth," *Science News* 111 (5 March 1977): 154.

7. Ibid.

gram, and in light of these earlier observed difficulties, one is left with the conclusion, in spite of evolutionary dogma to the contrary, that the available data indicate that the sun does not produce its energy by thermonuclear fusion and must not be very old. This finding reinstates gravitational collapse as a viable model for generating the sun's energy and rules out the possibility of the vast ages hoped for by proponents of Darwin's theory. With this in mind, a recent debate within the ranks of solar astronomers becomes quite intriguing, as we shall see next.

Is the Sun Shrinking?

Major newspapers across the country bannered this head-line: "The Sun Is Shrinking." The March 1980 Associated Press news story by Kevin McKean reported the results of research studies by solar specialist Jack Eddy of the Harvard-Smithsonian Center for Astrophysics and the National Center for Atmospheric Research and mathematician Aram Boornazian.[8] Through examination of records kept by the British Royal Observatory since 1750, Eddy and Boornazian concluded that the sun appears to be shrinking at a rate of about one-tenth of a percent per century.[9]

One characteristic common to all people is the tendency to notice and accept information that supports their own beliefs, values, biases, and so on. This is equally true of creationists and evolutionists. With this fact in mind, it is easy to imagine—given the considerations of the gravitational-collapse model of solar energy generation and results of the solar-neutrino experiments discussed above—how quickly recent-creationists noticed and grabbed hold of the Eddy and Boornazian findings.

8. *Wichita Eagle and Beacon,* op. cit.

9. John A. Eddy and Aram A. Boornazian, "Analyses of Historical Data Suggest Sun is Shrinking," *Physics Today* 32, No. 9 (September 1979): 17.

The creationist physicist Russell Akridge, for example, published an article shortly after the disclosure of the Eddy and Boornazian findings reporting calculations indicating that the earth could hardly be over a few thousand years old if the sun were shrinking at the reported rate.[10] Akridge also performed calculations showing that the suspected rate of solar shrinkage reported by Eddy and Boornazian would be more than enough to supply the 4×10^{26} watts of power actually produced by the sun.

Of course, just as recent-creationists were delighted by the possibility of another piece of evidence in support of their position and all too willing to accept it as verified fact, so evolutionists were extremely dubious and critical of Eddy and Boornazian's report. As one evolutionist critic put it, "This rate can *clearly* not be constant; if it were, the sun would shrink to a point in 100,000 years and would have been twice its present diameter 100,000 years ago."[11] (Emphasis was added.) Of course, if evolutionary theory is correct, such changes in the sun over a time span of only 100,000 years are impossible.

Spurred by grave doubts in the possibility of such a high rate of shrinkage as well as by normal scientific curiosity, evolutionist experts in this area of research sought to check Eddy and Boornazian's calculations with other observational means. Irwin I. Shapiro of M.I.T., for example, examined observational records (dating from 1736) of the time taken for Mercury to pass in front of the sun.[12] The Mercury-transit data showed no evidence of a decrease in the solar diameter and so raised doubts at least in regard to the rapid rate of shrinkage indicated by the Royal Observatory data.

Later, a group of scientists led by David W. Dunham of the International Occultation Timing Association, Silver Spring, Maryland, examined data gathered from 1715, 1976, and

10. Russell Akridge, "The Sun Is Shrinking," *Impact,* No. 82, April 1980 (Institute for Creation Research, 2716 Madison Ave., San Diego, Ca 92116).

11. Irwin I. Shapiro, "Is the Sun Shrinking?" *Science* 208 (4 April 1980): 51–53.

12. Ibid.

1979 on the size of the area of totality during solar eclipses.[13] In contrast to the Mercury-transit data examined by Shapiro, the solar-eclipse data examined by the Dunham group did show evidence of a small amount of shrinkage between 1715 and 1979. However, it was also found that the apparent amount of decrease in the sun's diameter was only about one-seventh of that reported by Eddy and Boornazian. More recently, J. H. Parkinson, of the Mullard Space Science Laboratory, reviewed the range of solar-eclipse and mercury-transit data and concluded that "there is no evidence for any secular change in the solar diameter."[14]

Conclusion

Is the sun truly shrinking? The answer is that at present we do not know. The data that have been gathered from a variety of different kinds of observations, including solar eclipses and transits of the planet Mercury as well as the optical evaluations utilized by Jack Eddy and Aram Boornazian, are subject to many known and unknown sources of error. Scientists engaged in this research are often operating near the limit of discernible effects in terms of the capability of our scientific instruments. It has been argued that this is especially true of the type of measurements used by Eddy and Boornazian to arrive at the original conclusion that the sun is shrinking.[15] Therefore, many subjective and judgmental factors, including one's bias on the issue of evolution vs. creation, are involved in trying to answer the question.

13. David W. Dunham, Sabatino Sofia, Alan D. Fiala, David W. Herald, and Paul M. Muller, "Observations of a probable change in the solar radius between 1715 and 1979," *Science* 210 (12 December 1980): 1243–1245.

14. John H. Parkinson, "New measurements of the solar diameter," *Nature* 304 (11 August 1983): 518–520.

15. John H. Parkinson, Leslie V. Morrison, and F. Richard Stephenson, "The constancy of the solar diameter over the past 250 years," *Nature* 288 (11 December 1980): 548–551.

One of the biggest problems in getting reliable, long-term data on the solar diameter is the possibility that observations gathered over many years may be subject to errors resulting from unknown changes in factors thought to be constant on the basis of the evolutionists' *assumption* that the cosmos is billions of years old. If the recent-creationists are correct in their analysis of the age of creation, many factors affecting solar-disk size estimates may be changing at a rate sufficient to invalidate those estimates.

The answer to the question of whether the sun is shrinking will have to await further research. Given the evidence from a number of sources indicating that nuclear fusion cannot be the mechanism by which the sun generates its power—leaving gravitational collapse as perhaps the only viable theory—it is a good bet that recent-creationists will continue to look for clear evidence that the sun is, indeed, shrinking.

7

The Vast Beyond

*The heavens are telling of the glory of God; And their
expanse is declaring the work of His hands.*

Ps. 19:1, NASB

To this point the discussion has generally been about outer-
space clocks in our own solar system. Soon our discussion will
get back down to earth and begin considering earthbound
clocks; but first let us examine some of the exciting things
that have been learned about the vast beyond of stars,
galaxies, and clusters of galaxies: intergalactic space.

As a biblical creationist, I believe that God created the
heavens and earth out of nothing (i.e., not out of any
preexisting matter) a few thousand years ago. Nowhere in the
Scriptures does it say exactly how old the creation is, but if
we calculate through the listed genealogies, we arrive at the
figure of about six thousand years. If the seven days of the
creation week described in the first chapter of Genesis are
understood as regular twenty-four-hour days, the figure of six
thousand years then applies to the whole of creation.

To many, the idea of a recent creation by the Word of God
is an incredible concept. Agreed, the concept *is* incredible.
However, in the area of ultimate origins, all the alternatives
are incredible. Consider, for example, the dominant evolutionist scenario for the beginning: the Big Bang.

According to the Big Bang concept all the matter of the
universe—all of reality—was once compressed into a tiny
ball. For some reason the tiny ball became unstable, explod-
ed, and turned into stars, planets, strawberries, cockroaches,
Good Humor wagons, committees, and this book.

A great portion of the resources and brainpower of modern
science is being poured into an effort to make this materialist
scenario sound plausible. The attempt has been monumental
and the results impressive, but the conflicting hard data are
mounting up, and it is time for people to begin pointing out
that "the emperor has no clothes." The view that the present
physical universe somehow created itself and is billions of

years old is contradicted by the growing weight of powerful physical evidence. The creation is not billions of years old; it is quite young.

The Mystery of Sirius B

In 1978 at Louisiana State University in Baton Rouge, a symposium of top scientists was held to discuss the issue of time and the age of the earth and cosmos.[1] Certain problems and paradoxes in the current conception of cosmic antiquity were explored by the scientists at this gathering.

Among the fascinating topics discussed was a puzzle known as the Sirius mystery. This mystery centers on a star named Sirius B, which is a type of star referred to as a "white dwarf." The problem stems from the fact that although ancient astronomers were also well acquainted with this star, unlike our present-day astronomers they described Sirius as red rather than white! Consider the following:

1. Egyptian hieroglyphs from 2000 b.c. described Sirius as red.

2. Cicero, writing in 50 b.c., stated that Sirius was red.

3. Seneca described Sirius as being redder than Mars, which he in turn described as redder than Jupiter.

4. The famous early astronomer Ptolemy in a.d. 150 listed Sirius as one of six red stars.

Modern astronomers are forced to accept the idea that within historical times Sirius B has transformed from a red giant to a white dwarf star. What is the problem with that? The mystery of Sirius B is that according to present conceptions of thermonuclear star radiation (see chapter 6), it should take at least 100,000 years for a red giant star to collapse into a white dwarf star. Something is obviously wrong with our present conception of how stars work.

1. Raphael G. Kazmann, "It's About Time: 4.5 Billion Years," *Geotimes*, September 1978, pp. 18–20.

The Field-Galaxy Mystery

Not long ago at a Fourth of July celebration, I looked on as hundreds of balloons were filled with helium and placed in a net enclosure. At the prescribed moment, the net was pulled away and the balloons released into the sky. As they drifted upward, they constituted a kind of clock in the sense that at the start they were all tightly clustered together. As they ascended, however, the cluster gradually broke up until after a while there were simply hundreds of individual balloons, each seemingly going its own way. The net had held all the balloons in a tight cluster for over an hour, but once the net was taken away, the balloon cluster began to dissipate rapidly.

Galaxies are clusters of millions and millions of stars. Many years ago astronomers thought there were two kinds of galaxies: cluster and field.[2] Cluster galaxies were those that existed in close gravitational proximity to other galaxies—in the same manner as the balloons shortly after the net was removed. Although such clusters of galaxies sometimes contain only a few galaxies, many of them contain millions. Field galaxies, on the other hand, were thought to be single galaxies, moving through space in relative independence and isolation—somewhat like the balloons after they had drifted for a time and no longer seemed associated with any other balloon or the cluster from which they had all dispersed.

Evolutionary scientists have long believed that galaxies and galaxy clusters are ten to twenty billion years old, but their studies of these incredible phenomena began to give rise to a baffling enigma some years ago. Observations indicated that insufficient mass existed in the galaxy clusters, too little to hold the clusters together. In most cases 80 to 90 percent of

2. Information on the field galaxy mystery is based on information provided by astrophysicist Harold Slusher in a talk presented at Wichita State University in April 1982.

the mass needed to obtain long-term gravitational stability was lacking. Of course, without gravitational stability the galaxy clusters would break up, just like the balloon cluster at the Fourth of July celebration.

Most disturbing from an evolutionary point of view were measurements that indicated the typical time for "breakup" or dissipation of the galaxy clusters was *at most* two to four million years. This, of course, would mean that the universe cannot be anything approaching the age required by the theory of evolution. To add to the mystery, exhaustive searches of the heavens have failed to turn up any field galaxies. If evolutionists are correct, and galaxy clusters have been around for ten to twenty billion years, then many galaxy clusters should have dissolved—and there ought to be an abundance of field galaxies. However, field galaxies are not to be found. Evolutionists have spared no effort in trying to resolve this dilemma for their theory.

The prime hope has been to find the "missing mass" necessary to provide the gravity to hold the clusters together and "keep the galaxies down on the farm," as Harold Slusher puts it. At first, scientists proposed that there might be a lot of hot hydrogen gas in the clusters that could provide enough mass to hold them together, but observations revealed that this was not the answer. Then they looked for cold hydrogen, but again not enough was found. Finally, with the advance of space technology, scientists could look for lukewarm hydrogen, but again not enough was found to hold the galaxies together.

When the hope of hydrogen gas as the answer to the "missing mass" problem faded, some began to suggest that black holes might be the answer. As Slusher points out, however, a very large number of black holes evenly distributed throughout the cluster would be needed, and this, of course, creates more problems for an evolutionist time scale than it solves. If black holes exist, they gobble up matter—including stars and galaxies. Thus, if there are large numbers of them running around, the galaxy clusters will be eaten up by their black holes instead of breaking up into isolated field galaxies. Black holes do not offer a solution.

Conclusion

One very simple answer does exist, and that is to take the data at face value. The clusters are not gravitationally bound and are breaking up just as they appear to be. The reason they still exist as clusters is that they have not existed long enough to dissipate. The absolute maximum age for most clusters is two to four million years, but a few small clusters have breakup times indicating a maximum age of only a few thousand years. Some two-member galaxies are so close that they are connected by trails of gas, and they are moving apart so rapidly they could not be more than a few thousand years old. Once again the evidence for age is found to be on the side of youth rather than antiquity.

8

The Speed of Light

Covering Thyself with light as with a cloak, Stretching
out heaven like a tent curtain.   Ps. 104:2, NASB

Of all the topics discussed in this book, the following is the
most far-reaching and revolutionary in its implications for a
relatively recent six-day creation as described in the Genesis
record. Interestingly, the account of this most amazing clock
of all begins with the fervent prayer of a perplexed young
man.

After becoming a Christian, an Australian named Barry
Setterfield, a student of physics and astronomy, began to
struggle with the obvious conflict between the biblical account of creation and the currently accepted cosmological
view he had learned during his scientific training.[1] In particular he had difficulty reconciling the Genesis implications of
a sudden and recent creation with the arguments and evidences that seemed to imply the vast antiquity of the earth
and cosmos. Most specifically he felt trapped logically by
what has become over the years the evolutionists' most
persuasive argument for an ancient origin of the universe—
the speed of light.

The Speed-of-Light Argument

The most powerful evolutionist "age argument" for most
thinking persons has been that based on the measured speed
of light and the time it would take light to travel from

1. The material in this chapter is based in part on information provided by Barry
Setterfield in a speech titled "The Velocity of Light and the Age of the Universe,"
presented at the 1983 National Creation Conference in Minneapolis, Minnesota. (A
tape of this talk may be obtained from the Bible-Science Association, 2911 E. 42nd
St., Minneapolis, MN 55406.) Information was also obtained from a technical
monograph of the same title by Barry Setterfield and obtainable from Creation Science
Foundation, P.O. Box 302, Sunnybank, Qld., 4109, Australia.

distant objects in the heavens. We hear of stars and galaxies that are believed to be millions and even billions of light-years from earth. Even if scientists are greatly mistaken in their views about the size of the universe and distance to the far reaches of the cosmos, surely it must be admitted that these distant objects are far in excess of a few thousand light-years away. If so, how can the entire universe be only a few thousand years old?

By far the most common creationist answer to the dilemma has been to suggest that when God created the distant stars he created "light trails" connecting them to the earth, to each other, and so forth. To the unbelieving skeptic, this is probably the most irritating argument in the creationist arsenal, and Barry Setterfield had grave reservations about accepting it.

The most unpalatable aspect of the created-light-trail argument is that it implies that much of what we see in the night sky never really happened, since it is a record of events that would have occurred before the creation of all things. The argument seems, on the surface at least, to lay God open to a legitimate charge of deception. Barry Setterfield began to look into the matter.

A Look at the Evidence

In the entire history of scientific investigation there have been less than a hundred published determinations (each made by averaging a number of separate measurements) of the speed of light. The first determination was reported by the Danish astronomer Roemer in 1675, and the second followed some fifty years later in 1728 and was made by the English astronomer Bradley. No more determinations were made until the mid-1800s, and from that time to the present, determinations of the speed of light have occurred fairly frequently. Although published measurements of the speed of light that have not been previously noted by researchers occasionally do turn up, these are almost all from the modern era. The pre-1940 data are thought by most experts to be complete. This point is vital, since it means that the examination made by Setterfield into the provocative question of light-speed decay is based upon *all* the evidence there is.

Barry Setterfield examined these data, and—much to his amazement and in spite of everything he had learned from his professors and textbooks—the figures showed a clear and distinct pattern of decay with the passage of time. The speed of light has not been constant; it was faster in the past.

Setterfield was astonished. Had anyone in the scientific community ever noticed this decay trend? He found the answer to be in the affirmative. There have been a number of scientists in the past who saw the trend and concluded that light must be slowing down. Articles to this effect have appeared in the scientific literature over the years. Nevertheless, the evolutionary scientific establishment has assumed the constancy of the speed of light in spite of the actual physical data.

An Incredible Discovery

At this point Setterfield began an extensive investigation into the light-speed evidence to find out more about the rate and parameters of the decay as well as other physical implications. The interested reader should obtain Setterfield's monograph on this topic, since it elaborates technical details and laymen's summaries far beyond the scope of this book. (It may be obtained from Creation Science Foundation, P.O. Box 302, Sunnybank, Qld., 4109, Australia.)

One of the first things Setterfield set out to do was to determine the best curve to fit the observed light-speed measurements. This would enable one to make projections back into the past and see what the speed of light was at earlier times and, more importantly for our purposes, to obtain an estimate of when the whole process began and thereby make an approximation of the age of the universe.

Of all the decay curves that could be fitted to the existing data, one stood out clearly as the best fit. Setterfield's jaw dropped as he viewed the curve. It indicated an origin of the universe about six thousand years ago—the traditional figure based on analysis of biblical chronologies and genealogies! At some point a little beyond 4000 B.C., the curve approaches infinite light speed and thus the ultimate origin.

Staggering Implications

Setterfield has devoted many years to researching this problem and testing out its theoretical and practical implications. There are far-reaching implications that go well beyond the scope of this chapter. Suffice it to say that this one factor potentially explains an astounding array of cosmic perplexities, including many earth formations and mineral deposits, water-erosion features on other planets such as Mars, anomalies in the inferred velocities of distant galaxies, the "echo of the Big Bang," and many others.

From the standpoint of the age issue, one extremely important implication needs to be explained. The principal method scientists use to determine ages of matter involves various types of radioactive decay. The main reason most scientists (as well as lay people) give for accepting evolutionary claims for vast geologic ages is related to the results of various radioactive dating procedures involving such materials as carbon 14, uranium-lead, and potassium-argon. If certain assumptions are granted, all such methods indicate ages far in excess of a few thousand years.

In the past, recent-creationists have attacked this central fortress of the evolutionists' ages concept by challenging these necessary assumptions. This approach has been fairly success-

ful, owing to the tenuous nature of many of the radioactive-
dating assumptions. However, the discovery that the speed of
light has been slowing down through history raises a whole
new and devastating problem for all radioactive-dating methods, since a key factor in all such rates of decay is the speed of
light. Physicists know that the rate of decay for radioactive
elements is directly related to the speed of light. The faster
the speed of light, the more rapid the decay of radioactive
elements, and vice versa. This means that all dating calculations published in the past must be refigured with the
corrected and ever-decreasing value for light speed. When
this is done, all radioactive dates fall within a time frame of a
few thousand years!

To see why radioactive dates are so drastically reduced,
consider a simple example of a rock thought by modern
calculations to be four billion years old. The four-billion-year
figure assumes, however, that the speed of light was the same
in the past as it is now and thus that the rate of radioactive
decay was the same in the past as it is today. When scientists
infer from certain measurements that a considerable amount
of radioactive decay has occurred in a rock, they assume that
the decay process has always proceeded at today's rate and
therefore that billions of years were required for the rock to
reach its present condition.

Now we introduce the finding that light traveled much
faster in the past—and *if* light traveled faster in the past, the
radioactive-decay process in the rock sample was also proceed-
ing more rapidly in the past. Thus the amount of decay that
scientists thought would take four billion years to accomplish
is now seen to take only six thousand years. The new estimate
of the rock's age is thereby dramatically reduced. All radioactive-
decay dates are brought into the recent-creation time frame
by Setterfield's results.

Current Status of Setterfield's Work

Setterfield's work with the speed of light is understandably controversial. Even many recent-creationists have been very cautious about this revolutionary concept and take an almost it's-too-good-to-be-true posture. For his part, Setterfield has continued his research and sought every opportunity to debate and discuss his findings with fellow scientists. To date no one has been able to debunk the findings, and corroborations of Setterfield's work seem to be piling up.

As one example, Setterfield has examined historical measurements of over a dozen other so-called fundamental atomic constants that would be related to the speed of light. A number of these postulated constants are independent of light-speed changes because of mutually canceling factors and thus should really have constant values through history. Others *are* tied to light speed and should, in fact, be showing the same decreasing historical trend found with speed-of-light measurements. Still others relate to the speed of light in an inverse manner and would be expected to have increased historically.

Astonishingly, and in spite of the fact that all of these fundamental parameters are—as with the speed of light—assumed by modern astronomers to be constants, every one of them shows the exact historical trend predicted by Setterfield. The odds against such matching data trends in support of Setterfield's theory occurring by mere chance are astronomical. It is easy to see why this work is generating a lot of interest. The evidence keeps piling up. The universe is young!

9

Back Down to Earth

. . . the earth is full of thy riches. So is this great and
wide sea, wherein are things creeping innumerable, both
small and great beasts.   Ps. *104: 24–25*

Our own home, earth, is the place scientists know the most
about, and a great abundance of "clocks" have been found all
around us. One good example was the "fossil" meteorite
clock explained in chapter 2. A few clocks that we hear about
all the time have been interpreted in such a way that they
seem to indicate long cosmic ages. The most common are the
various types of radioactive-decay clocks.

The Problems with Radioactive Clocks

As was seen in the previous chapter, however, the startling
discovery that the speed of light has been slowing down
through history changes the whole picture regarding radioactive clocks. It can now be seen that they do not indicate vast
ages as formerly thought, since—as physicists well know—
the speed at which a radioactive decay clock runs is directly
related to the speed at which light travels.

Even before the uncovering of the light-speed data, recent-
creationists had uncovered much evidence to indicate that
there was something amiss with the standard evolutionist
interpretation of radioactive clocks. For example, the com-
monly cited uranium-lead decay sequence gives off helium as
a by-product. Yet not nearly "enough" helium is present in
the atmosphere, if this radioactive process has been occurring
for millions and billions of years, in the manner claimed by
evolutionists. In fact, there is only a few thousand years'
worth of helium in the atmosphere, even if all of it came
from this source. For this reason recent-creationists have often

cited the amount of atmospheric helium as a clock indicating a young earth.[1]

Also, large numbers of radioactive-dating discrepancies and anomalies can be cited to indicate that unknown factors and faulty assumptions may be at work. In 1968 scientists applied radiometric dating to some rocks that were *known* to be less than 170 years old. They knew this because the rocks had been formed by a volcanic eruption in 1800 on the island of Hualalai in Hawaii. The radioactive ages determined for these 170-year-old rocks ranged from 160 million to 3 billion years.[2] Obviously, something is wrong with this method. We will deal with this subject further in chapter 11.

A Whale on Its Tail

More problematic than radiometric clocks to a young-earth position are certain geological features that seem to require long ages to form. By no means do creationist scientists have all the answers to these dilemmas, but more is being learned all the time.

One of the most intriguing examples of a dilemma for which new discoveries are leading to a solution involves a

1. At first glance, the low amount of atmospheric helium seems to create a dilemma for Barry Setterfield's model involving decay in the speed of light, since faster light speed and corresponding faster uranium-lead decay should produce helium at a faster rate. Thus, whether the radioactive decay occurred over millions of years or only a few thousand, there should be the same amount of helium by-product produced.

But where is the helium? The answer may be that in Setterfield's model it is predicted that the radioactive elements were originally confined deep in the earth's interior and only later intruded near the earth's surface as a result of catastrophic events. Helium is known to be *extremely* soluble in the magma of the earth's interior. Even under circumstances whereby the molten magma erupts through to the earth's surface, it will not release the helium readily. There are many known intrusions of igneous rock (cooled magma) that contain substantial amounts of helium without nearby uranium sources.

2. John G. Funkhouser and John J. Naughton, "Radiogenic Helium and Argon in Ultramafic Inclusions from Hawaii," *Journal for Geophysical Research* 73, No. 14 (15 July 1968): 4601–4607.

type of microscopic sea creature known as a diatom. Since this tiny creature has a shell that does not decompose when it dies, the shells of dead diatoms gradually settle down to the ocean bottoms and, under appropriate conditions, form deposits called diatomaceous earth. Such deposits can run to hundreds of feet of thickness and be remarkably free of other contaminates. The dilemma for the recent-creationist is how in the world such deposits can form in a relatively short period of time.

Although these features seem to present a considerable problem for the idea of a young earth, clear indications are in evidence that there must be a solution.

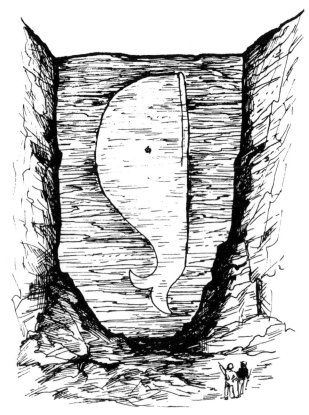

(Artist's conception of the whale on its tail)

At a diatomaceous-earth quarry in Lompoc, California, a remarkable discovery was made during mining operations in 1976.[3] Workers of the Dicalite Division of Grefco Corporation uncovered the fossil skeleton of a baleen whale. The whale fossil is standing on end in the quarry and is being exposed gradually as the diatomite is mined. Estimates are that the fossil is about eighty feet long.

What does this find mean? In a phrase, it means that this formation could not have been built up gradually over millions of years. The billions of tiny diatom shells making up the formation had to be deposited in a very short period of time. Here is why—

A creature that dies does not normally become a fossil. In order to do so it must be buried deeply and quickly in wet sediment to seal if off from the atmosphere, bacteria, and so forth. Otherwise it will simply rot. Thus, one can be confident that the eighty-foot portion of the formation containing the whale had to be deposited quickly.

In addition, if deposition of the diatoms was sporadic, with long periods of time separating brief periods of rapid deposition, there ought to be clear lines of erosional separation in the formation rather than a smooth and continuous conformity. Since there are no such erosional lines in the deposit, the indication is that not only the eighty-foot portion containing the fossil whale, but the remainder of the deposit as well, must have been deposited quickly. Other evidences point in the same direction for other kinds of deposits.

A Sword in a Stone

In the famous legend, Arthur shows that he is righteous and true by pulling Excalibur from a stone. A modern

3. "Workers Find Whale in Diatomaceous Earth Quarry," *Chemical and Engineering News,* 11 October 1976, p. 40.

Excalibur of sorts is found under the imposing name *polystrate fossils*. The word means "many layers," and it refers to fossils—usually tree trunks—that cut through two or more layers of sedimentary rock. How do these sword-in-a-stone fossils indicate that the earth may not be as old as evolutionists believe?

To the average person, the most powerful witness to claims of vast prehistoric ages is the testimony of sometimes thousands of feet of sedimentary-rock layers and the fossils they contain. The sight of the Grand Canyon with its layer upon layer of sedimentary rock seems to imply the requirement of vast amounts of time. Evolutionists believe and propose that each layer represents an ancient world that long since perished. Recent-creationists, on the other hand, believe that these rock layers were all deposited quickly under catastrophic conditions in the relatively recent past. The occurrence of polystrate fossils in numerous places around the world is one dramatic piece of evidence that the recent-creationists may be right.

In order to see why, remember that fossil formation requires rapid burial and sealing from atmospheric and surface elements. Any organic material, such as wood, that is so exposed will not turn into a fossil. Rather, it will rot. Therefore, just as with the whale in the diatomite deposit, the entire length of a fossil tree trunk had to be buried quickly in order for it to fossilize.

However, in polystrate fossils, these tree trunks extend vertically and are incorporated into rock layers supposedly laid down in epochs separated by millions of years of time. The most obvious and straightforward interpretation of these fossils is that the sedimentary layers engulfing them were laid down in rapid succession during a single catastrophe in the past. They constitute a sort of frozen clock from the past, indicating that terrible things occurred—not over millions of years but very quickly. The earth's sedimentary-rock layers are not a testimony of life's long struggle upward but a witness of sudden terror and judgment.

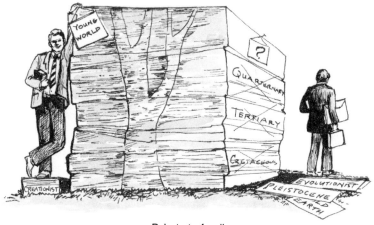

Polystrate fossil

Conclusion

Although the details of many deposits, erosional features, formations, and so forth, present numerous mysteries and dilemmas for the concept of recent creation as described in the Book of Genesis, much exciting work is being done. New and amazing answers and evidences are turning up all the time. Since the hard evidence we already have indicates that there must be answers, creationists will continue to look for them. As Walter Lang of the Bible-Science Association is fond of saying, "If you just give science enough time it will finally catch up with the Bible." I trust this book will help the reader to be more fully assured of that fact.

10

The Top That Reeled

. . . The earth shall reel to and fro like a drunkard.
Isa. 24:20

Biblical creationists consider the Genesis account of the flood in the time of Noah to be genuine history. According to the Genesis record, the flood was worldwide in its impact and occurred around 2200 to 2300 B.C.

Christians have traditionally pointed to the extensive sedimentary-rock layers with their numerous fossil remains as being the principal evidence for the flood. Another line of verification that has been put forward is the reports over the centuries by explorers and adventurers who claim to have sighted the remains of the great ark still at rest on Mount Ararat. The present chapter reports on some exciting discoveries by an Australian astronomer that provide new evidence for the Genesis flood.

Evidence from the Ancients

An intriguing mystery began to unravel with some routine research work by the late Australian astronomer George Dodwell. The thread of the mystery would lead Dodwell from some puzzling astronomical observations recorded by ancient astronomers to evidence for a dramatic alteration in the earth's axial tilt in the recent past and a surprising confirmation of the historical trustworthiness of the Bible.

Astronomer Dodwell was examining lists of winter/summer solstice shadow measurements (length of sun's noonday shadow on the longest and shortest day of the year) as recorded and left by ancient astronomers from as long ago as three thousand years. The mystery begins with the well-known fact that there seems something is wrong with these measurements. An *apparent* inaccuracy is present in these data that is totally out of character with the well-documented meticulousness of the remainder of the ancients' astronomical records and observations. Although the recorded shadow lengths are correct in respect to latitude position, they are wrong in respect to what modern astronomers think should be the axis alignment with the sun. What makes the idea of errors in these measurements odd is the fact that the ancient astronomers saw a religious significance in their astronomical calculations and therefore took them very seriously. Errors in their work beyond those imposed by the limitations of ancient observing methods are extremely unlikely. Also, the correctness of the latitude measurements give credibility to the accuracy of the axis-alignment data. Dodwell thought the "error explanation" of these figures must be wrong.

As he pondered the data, a decision was made to graph the measurements recorded by the ancients and compare them to what modern astronomers suppose they should have been, based upon reverse projections from present-day planetary alignments and motions. When Dodwell did so, he found that the ancient measurements formed a distinct pattern of increasing discrepancy with modern projections as one went further back in time. The data also fit a curve with which Dodwell was quite familiar. It was the curve of recovery for a spinning top that is struck by an outside force. Dodwell began to suspect that the problem had nothing to do with the accuracy of the ancient recordings but rather with our modern conception of how the earth and sun were aligned in the past. A dramatic and *recent* change in that alignment must have occurred.

Even so, Dodwell was puzzled by what lay before him. What did it all mean? The calculations on his desk lay untouched for two years while he pondered that question. When their import was finally realized, the impact of the realization led Dodwell on a totally unexpected turn to a deeper commitment to Christianity and the historical trustworthiness of the Bible. These commitments were to occupy his time and energy through the remainder of his life. Dodwell's scientific efforts, stimulated by what he became convinced were not erroneous measurements by the ancients, were never fully compiled in his lifetime but fortunately are now being made known through efforts of the Australian-based Creation Science Foundation.[1]

Three Additional Mysteries

What did Dodwell discover? George Dodwell had caught hold of an intriguing puzzle. Isolated anomalies in the date calculations for various historical events began to fall into a surprising pattern. Dodwell's line of research led him to a consideration of three other well-documented dating enigmas relating to (1) the ancient astronomer, Eudoxus; (2) Stonehenge; and (3) the Egyptian Solar Temple of Amen-Ra. The common thread in these three cases is that, like the ancient solstice shadow measurements, they indicate there is something wrong with our modern assumptions of how the earth's axis aligned with the heavens in past times.

Eudoxus

Eudoxus was a well-known Greek mathematician, geographer, and astronomer who lived from about 400 to 347 B.C. Among the astronomical observations made by Eudoxus is a careful description of the North Celestial Pole (the point in the sky around which the stars appear to rotate and thus the position marking the alignment of the earth's axis). The

1. Material for this chapter was obtained from the following sources: A talk entitled, "Astronomical Evidence for the Flood," presented by Barry Setterfield at the 1983 National Creation Conference in Minneapolis, Minnesota (tapes of this presentation may be obtained from the Bible-Science Association, 2911 E. 42nd St., Minneapolis, MN 55406) and two articles published in Ex Nihilo (P.O. Box 18339, Tucson, AZ 85731)—Carl Wieland, "An Asteroid Tilts the Earth," Ex Nihilo, January 1983, pp. 12–14; and Barry Setterfield, "An Asteroid Tilts the Earth?" Ex Nihilo, April 1983, pp. 6–8.

problem is that on the basis of reverse projections from modern measurements of the earth's axis, orbit, and so forth, the observations of Eudoxus do not fit the time of 350 B.C. (at which they were made) but rather a time some 1,600 years earlier, or about 1900 B.C. If Eudoxus did make his observations in 350 B.C., as he claimed, there is something seriously wrong with our present-day procedure of projecting directly back from current astronomical alignments to determine what the alignments should have been at particular times in the past.

Stonehenge

Another excellent example is Stonehenge, an ancient man-made construction consisting of huge stone slabs arranged in circular patterns and situated on the Salisbury Plain in southern England. In ancient times Stonehenge was used for astronomical observations in the context of religious rites and ceremonies.

On the basis of archaeological evidence and considerations, Stonehenge was for many years associated with the ancient Druid cult and thus dated at about 350 B.C. Modern astro-

Stonehenge

nomical research, however, has upset the simple conclusion of associating Stonehenge with the Druids, and the dating for the monument is now set much earlier—between 1500 to 1900 B.C. The reason for the change in dating is that the astronomical solstice measurements, which Stonehenge was built to observe, would not—according to reverse projections from current planetary positions—have been possible in 350 B.C. but only at the earlier date.

By this time the pattern was becoming clear to Dodwell, and he was beginning to see that the problem was with modern astronomical dating. A dramatic event had occurred, which was not being accounted for in the calculations. Dodwell now believed that the archaeologists had been right all along in dating Stonehenge at about 350 B.C.

Egyptian Solar Temple of Amen-Ra, Karnak

A final and apparently conclusive piece of the puzzle is found in connection with the Solar Temple of Amen-Ra at Karnak in Egypt. This temple was built during the time of the Pharaohs near or some time after 2000 B.C., and it was the site of a most impressive religious ceremony known as the "manifestation of Ra" (sun god).

The Egyptian Pharaohs claimed to be divine, and the once-a-year ceremony at Amen-Ra was designed to emphasize the point. At the center of the temple was a darkened sanctuary filled with gold and other magnificently jeweled decorations. Connecting to the outside from the sanctuary was a long narrow hallway. As the ancient summers drew near, the days grew longer and longer. The sun was positioned in the sky a little more northward each day, until it reached the most northerly position of its annual progression, marking the summer solstice and longest day of the year. On that longest day and only on that day, the setting sun was far enough north to shine down the long corridor of Amen-Ra and flood the sanctuary with light.

Solar Temple of Amen-Ra at Karnak, Egypt (Sketch from an unknown artist's rendering)

On that glorious day, the priests and other important persons would gather along the corridor, while Pharaoh stood in the darkened inner sanctuary. As the sun sank, it shone down the long corridor, and Pharaoh was suddenly swallowed up in the blinding brilliance. The sun god Ra and the god Pharaoh had become one—a most impressive ceremony, except for one tiny problem.

According to modern astronomical calculations, during the time of the temple's historical use, the sun would not have reached far enough north to shine down the corridor and into the sanctuary. Yet we know from ancient hieroglyphic writings that the sun did indeed shine into the sanctuary. Obviously there is something wrong with our modern astronomical calculations, according to which you would have to go back to at least 4000 B.C. for the manifestation-of-Ra ceremony to be possible.

That Strange Curve of Observations

When George Dodwell sought to solve the mysterious discrepancy between historical records and modern astronomy, he reached some startling conclusions. Earlier it was pointed out that he made a graph of the solstice shadow-length observations recorded by the ancients. When he constructed a mathematical curve to fit the observations, he made some important discoveries.

First, the curve had a point of origin dating at about 2345 B.C. He concluded that something dramatic must have occurred at that time.

Second, the curve determined by Dodwell cross-checked with the proper archaeological dates for Eudoxus, Stonehenge, and the Solar Temple of Amen-Ra. Dodwell's astronomical curve gave correct dates for these instances, thus tending to validate his calculations.

Third, as previously stated, Dodwell recognized the pattern

of the curve. He realized that the path of the curve matched to a remarkable degree of detail the recovery path of a spinning top that is struck from the outside and returns to a new position of spinning equilibrium.

The realization of these factors stunned Dodwell, for they indicated that something had happened to the earth in 2345 B.C. to cause it to tilt from its axis. Following that sudden and dramatic tilt, the earth began to wobble like a spinning top and gradually recovered to a new axial tilt. Our modern reverse projections give inaccurate historical dates because they fail to take this fact into account. Most important in all this for Dodwell was the recognition that the 2345 B.C. date for the tilting of the earth's axis coincides with the historical date of the Genesis flood, as based upon the study of biblical chronologies.

Asteroid Impact

Dodwell compiled an impressive body of data in support of the possibility that a heretofore unknown change in the tilt of the earth's axis occurred around 2345 B.C. Unaware of this change in the earth's rotational axis, many modern astronomers have been unable to match date estimates based on reverse astronomical projections with verified historical benchmarks. The calculations were thus flawed and gave date estimates for ancient events that are much too early. On the basis of Dodwell's research, it will now be possible to correct these astronomical dating procedures so that they yield valid results.

More importantly for us, Dodwell's discoveries provide evidence for the truth of the biblical record of world history. His findings support not only the historical fact of the flood but its occurrence at the time indicated by the Bible. In addition, Dodwell's research indicates that at the time of God's judgment on Noah's generation, there was a major realignment of the earth's axis. As to what might have caused such a tilt, Dodwell was not certain, but he came to believe that it was caused by the impact of an asteroid in what is now the Pacific Ocean.

The notion of such an impact is difficult to confirm and presents some nasty difficulties. Regarding this idea, another Australian astronomer, Barry Setterfield (see chapter 8), has remarked to the effect that if such a massive asteroid did, in fact, hit the earth, "the miracle is not that all of humanity perished in the great flood but that Noah and his family survived." It nevertheless remains an intriguing possibility and might explain some otherwise puzzling mysteries in the fossil record.

The Mammoths of the Northern Tundra

Among the most curious of archaeological mysteries are the vast beds of perfectly preserved fossils frozen in the northern tundras. Buried beneath the northern tundras of Siberia and Alaska lie the remains of thousands of frozen animals, including the now-extinct mammoth. In some cases the carcasses are preserved to such a degree that their flesh is still edible, usually only by bears and wolves but in a few reported instances by men. Today these northern tundras are cold and barren wastelands, but we know that in the past the climate was much warmer. Fossil evidence has been found of plants that grow today as far south as Mexico. At one time these tundras were covered with lush vegetation.

It is a mystery how so many mammoths and other animals could have been rapidly buried and preserved in cold storage, for the climate was warm at the time they were living. One such perfectly preserved carcass was found near the Beresovka River in Siberia in 1901.[2] Well-preserved plant fragments

2. Jody Dillow, "The Catastrophic Deep-Freeze of the Beresovka Mammoth," *Creation Research Society Quarterly* 14 (June 1977): 5–12.

were found in the mouth and between the teeth of the mammal, indicating the suddenness with which it met its death. Inside the mammoth's stomach, twenty-four pounds of excellently preserved vegetation was recovered. The mammoth's remarkably preserved state indicates that at the time of death there was a cataclysmic occurrence that produced both a rapid burial of the creature and a sudden and permanent drop in the temperature. Recent studies of the temperature parameters required to account for the state of preservation of the Beresovka mammoth reveal that "the animal must have frozen to death in mid-summer by being suddenly overcome by an outside temperature below −150° F."[3]

> . . . for the Beresovka mammoth, some violent climatic upheaval is the only explanation for these remains. The animal was peacefully grazing on summer buttercups in late July and within one half hour of ingestion of his last lunch, he was overcome by temperatures in excess of −150° F . . . whatever climatic upheaval caught him, permanently changed the climatic conditions of the tundra.[4]

In an attempt to relate the remarkable tundra fossils to Dodwell's concept of asteroid impact, Carl Wieland of Australia writes as follows:

> Even the evolutionists have sought to suggest that impact from outer space has been responsible for extinctions such as that of the dinosaurs. They have even produced theoretical models which predict that if a large object did smash into the ocean, a massive jet of superheated steam would be shot into the upper atmosphere, where it would be superchilled to form a layer of ice crystals which would block out the sunlight, and produce catastrophic climatic effects.
> But this impact idea helps explain other more puzzling

3. Ibid., p. 5.
4. Ibid., p. 12.

features. In order to push the earth's axis into its present position, the asteroid had to be coming from a particular direction. The snap frozen mammoths of Alaska and Siberia are right in the path of the jet of spray which would have been shot high into the atmosphere to supercool below freezing and fall to earth in these places, in addition to freezing effects of sunblocking mentioned earlier. The North Pole (which, as the world's driest spot, was not formed by snow falling slowly over time) is also in the path of any ice dump from this effect. World cooling would have followed this to produce widespread glaciation which has been melting back since that time.[5]

Continental Plates, Precipitates and Diatoms

Certain geologic features and characteristics might also be more clearly understood if Dodwell's suspicion of asteroid collision were proved to be tenable. Such impact on a scale large enough to tilt the earth's axis would result in a good deal of fracturing of the earth's crust. This fracturing could account for the recently discovered continental plates, which are apparently not existent on Venus and Mars.

Asteroid impact with subsequent crustal fracturing might also account for some of the puzzling precipitate deposits, such as were mentioned in chapter 9. Deep crust fracture would result in a lot of molten intrusion from the earth's interior. Such massive heated intrusion into the oceans might well result in rapid deposition of such minerals as limestone as cooling occurred. Massive and virtually pure limestone beds are difficult to explain on the basis of any known process operating today.

5. Wieland, "An Asteroid Tilts the Earth," p. 13.

Conclusion

We discussed the diatomaceous-earth deposits in chapter 9 and pointed out how they created an enigma for the recent-creation position. Nevertheless, such fossil evidence as the "whale on its tail" strongly suggests that the formation of these deposits had to occur rapidly under catastrophic circumstances. Asteroid impact might provide the answer. The heat produced by the impact itself—plus the heat and pollution produced by wide-scale intrusion from the earth's interior brought about by crustal fracture—would result in a "snowfall" of tiny shells to the bottom of the ocean floor as soon as the turbulence subsided. The diatomaceous-earth deposit at Lompoc, California, may have been part of the aftermath of such a collision.

11

Creation Stopwatches

*Behold, thou has made my days as an handbreadth; and
mine age is as nothing before thee.*   *Ps. 39:5*

In considering the age of the cosmos, one important difference between the evolutionist and creationist positions needs
to be discussed. The evolutionist stance maintains that all
features of the present universe have come into existence
through the operation of the scientifically observed regulari-
ties and processes we see operating today. The creationist, on
the other hand, contends that these observed processes cannot
account for the creation of the cosmos but are merely characteristic of its post-creation operation. This difference leads to a
major break between the two camps as to what constitutes
the most valid clocks for estimating the age of the universe.
To understand this difference, we may examine an Adam-and-
Eve illustration.

Adam and Eve and Carvings on Trees

If the Genesis account is regarded as historical narrative,
then Adam and Eve are seen as sudden and "mature" cre-
ations. They are also seen as inhabiting a mature world that
is finished and waiting for them. From a creationist view-
point, it would be very misleading to try to estimate the age
of the world by examining the developmental level of Adam
and such other *primary* features of the creation as size of trees,
amount of foliage, and so on.

On the other hand, with the passage of time, certain
secondary features would come into existence as a result of
interactions taking place between primary aspects of creation.
For instance, Adam might carve "Adam loves Eve" inside a
heart on a tree. This carving would be a secondary feature,
and if it could be dated by some scientific process, a
creationist would have a relatively high degree of confidence
in the outcome. Such dating would not, of course, tell us

how old the world is, but it would tell us that it must be at least as old as the tree carving. In contrast, the evolutionist would maintain that everything existing in the universe had to come about through a regular developmental process. Since no distinction between primary and secondary features is recognized, the developmental age of Adam would be given equal weight with the tree carving.

Application to Radioactive Dating

When evolutionists estimate the age of the universe at 10 to 20 billion years and the earth at 4.5 billion years, they use features that creationists would tend to regard as primary and therefore suspect as a measuring device. The estimate of 10 or 20 billion years for the age of the universe, for example, is derived in major part from estimates of the size of the universe. However, from a creationist point of view, the size of the universe and the age of the universe are independent. You cannot estimate one from the other.

The 4.5-billion-year estimate for the earth's age is derived by the evolutionist partly from the radioactive parent-daughter element ratios in the basement rocks of the earth's crust. Since these bedrocks are assumed to have formed early in the earth's evolutionary formation, their developmental states are taken as good age indicators. Again, however, from a creationist point of view, these radioactive ratios might be the least dependable age indicators. Many of the radioactive daughter elements, which take millions and billions of years to form under present-day conditions, are necessary or at least useful to human life. Creationists cannot imagine that a rich supply of these elements was not present at the beginning, and so using them to estimate age would be like Adam trying to guess the time since creation by measuring the depth of the topsoil in the Garden of Eden. Such things are primary features of creation and not valid estimators of age.

Radiohalos: An Amazing Discovery in Colorado

Among the world's leading experts on radiometric dating is Robert V. Gentry, formerly a head researcher in chemistry at the Oak Ridge National Laboratory. As a biblical creationist, Gentry kept the distinction between primary and secondary features of nature very much in mind as he set out to tackle the age question. Would it be possible to find secondary radiometric clocks that would logically have to have been "set at zero" at some point after the formation of the earth?

Gentry's search for such secondary radiometric clocks led him to the study of microscopic bits of radioactive material that are frequently found imbedded in different types of rock formations. The importance of these tiny intrusions to the age issue will become apparent shortly. Among the formations studied by Gentry are coal deposits in the Colorado Plateau, believed by evolutionists to be hundreds of millions of years old.[1]

At some time in the past in the Colorado Plateau, a great deal of forest vegetation became buried in thick, wet sediment. Buried tree trunks first of all became saturated with water. Suspended in the water were numerous microscopic mineral bits including uranium, which is radioactive. As water soaked into the porous woody material of the trees, some of the microscopic bits of uranium were also transported in and became lodged inside the trees. In the course of time, heat and pressure would affect the buried tree trunks and other forest materials, turning them into coal. Once the coalification process was completed, the uranium bits would be permanently sealed in the rock and—in the sense of providing a radiometric clock—"set at zero."

As a radioactive uranium bit decays, radiation extends in

1. Robert V. Gentry, et al., "Radiohalos in Coalified Wood: New Evidence Relating to the Time of Uranium Introduction and Coalification," *Science* 194 (15 October 1976): 315–317.

all directions into the surrounding coal for a small yet precise distance determined by the particle energy of the radiation. Over time this emitted radiation will change the color of the coal, forming a distinct sphere around the bit of uranium in the center. These tiny spheres of discolored rock surrounding a microscopic radioactive center are termed "radiohalos." Such radiohalos are Robert Gentry's specialty.

Uranium's Radiohalo Clocks

A number of secondary clocks can be identified in relation to these radiohalos. The two most obvious uses are (1) the precise dating of the radioactive center itself; and (2) the more general dating of the discolored area or halo surrounding the microscopic core.

Regarding the radioactive center, a bit of uranium has at some time in the past, before the wood material was hardened into coal, migrated into its present position. As the uranium bit undergoes radioactive decay, a form of lead is created. Once the coal has hardened and the uranium bit has been cemented into a fixed position, this lead isotope begins to accumulate at the site.

Scientists can now carefully examine the radioactive center to measure the ratio of the uranium "parent element" to the lead "daughter element." This ratio gives a fairly precise estimate of how long the decay process has been going on at that site and thus how old the coal formation is. Gentry has found that the uranium/lead ratios in the Colorado Plateau coal formation indicate that this formation is only a few thousand years old. To quote Gentry:

> Such extraordinary values admit the possibility that both the initial U (uranium) infiltration and coalification could possibly have occurred within the past several thousand years.[2]

2. Ibid., p. 316–317.

and again:

> . . . these ratios raise some crucial questions regarding the
> antiquity of these geologic formations and about the time
> required for coalification.[3]

As a validation of the uranium/lead dating of the radioactive center, the halo or discolored area surrounding the central
bit can also be examined. Gentry has found that the halos in
the Colorado formation are in an early stage of development,
again indicating that the coal deposit is quite young.

Polonium Halos: A Creation Stopwatch

In addition to the uranium halos, Gentry has also found
polonium halos in the Colorado Plateau formation. These add
an exciting dimension in that they offer evidence that the
time required to form the coal was extremely short. Scientists
now know that under proper conditions coal and oil can be
formed very quickly. Coal has been synthesized in the laboratory in about twenty minutes and oil in about two hours.
Gentry's work with polonium halos has provided evidence
that coal can also form in natural situations in a relatively
short period of time.

Polonium is a high-energy isotope with a short life span
(or half-life, as scientists call it). It forms a halo in a very
short amount of time before it becomes inactive. Many of
these halos in the Colorado formation are not spherical but
have been compressed and flattened out. This flattening
indicates that the halo developed when the coal was just
forming and was still somewhat soft. A spherical halo developed,
but then, as the coal became compressed and hardened, the
halo was flattened.

3. Ibid., p. 317.

Gentry's data indicate that the amount of time involved in the formation of these coal deposits was less than twenty-five to fifty years, probably much less. The basis for this estimate is the presence of fascinating dual halos around a single center in which one halo is flattened and the other is perfectly round. The flattened halos are of a type that would form in six months to a year. The round halos are of a type that would form in twenty-five to fifty years. Thus, the coal had to be hardened and in its present shape well within the

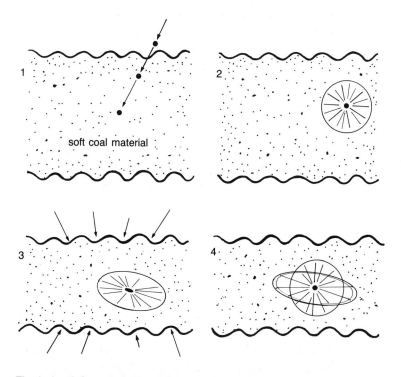

The logic of Gentry's interpretation of the dual halos can be summarized as follows: (1) a radioactive bit migrates into the soft woody material and becomes lodged in a fixed position; (2) within a few months a high-energy isotope present in the radioactive center produces a spherical halo; (3) the woody material is compressed and hardens into coal, flattening the initial radioactive halo; and (4) a second isotope present in the radioactive bit produces a second halo over a period of several years. This second halo retains its spherical shape, and thus the dual halos, one flattened and one spherical, are now in place.

twenty-five-to-fifty-year span in order for the spherical halo
to retain its form.

Work with the Earth's Basement Rocks

In addition to his work with coalified wood, Gentry has
also done extensive research with polonium halos in the
earth's "precambrian" granites, or basement rocks. This research has led to an incredible enigma for the evolutionary
model of earth's history. In the evolutionary scenario, the
precambrian granites represent the oldest rock layers and
were laid down millions of years before life began on earth.
As Gentry explains the theory:

> . . . a "protoearth" first condensed out of the gases of a solar
> nebula and was subsequently heated to a near-molten condi-
> tion about 4.5 billion years ago by gravitational contraction
> and radioactivity. In the scenario, different types of crustal
> rocks are presumed to have slowly crystallized as the earth
> gradually cooled over vast periods of time.[4]

The question Gentry has raised for evolutionists is how the
polonium bits and their resulting halos came to be in these
basement granites. The dilemma of finding polonium halos
in precambrian granite is similar to that posed by the
presence of a ship in a bottle. In order for the ship to get into
the bottle, the bottle must be broken, but if the bottle is
broken to get the ship inside, it cannot be put back together
in its unbroken form. In the analogy with polonium halos
and precambrian granite, the bottle represents the granite,
and the ship represents the polonium halo. How did the

4. "The fingerprints of God: Interview with Robert V. Gentry," *Ministry*, November
1981, pp. 20–21.

polonium and its resultant halos come to be in the granite?

Since polonium is a by-product or "daughter element" in the decay chain of uranium, evolutionists had always assumed that the polonium sites would always be associated with nearby uranium in some way. Gentry's research, however, has shown that this is not the case. The polonium sites are frequently isolated from any uranium source.

If there is no uranium close by, the only other possibility is that the polonium bits migrated into the granite from a remote uranium source. If this were the case, however, the migration would have to be *very rapid* because of the short half-life of polonium. Rapid migration of the polonium bits would only be possible if (1) the granite were in a molten form; or (2) tiny cracks were present in the rock, allowing access to the intrusion sites. Gentry's research reveals that generally there are no such cracks present to allow polonium entry. This leaves only the possibility that the granite was still in a molten form at the time of polonium intrusion. But this is impossible—because if the granite were in the molten state necessary to allow polonium intrusion, no perfect polonium halo could form!

The Argument for Creation's Stopwatch

The enigma is this: If the granite is hardened, the polonium cannot travel to its intrusion location. But if the granite is *not* hardened, no halo can form. Therefore, Gentry argues that the time lapse from a permeable, molten state to the present rock state for these precambrian granites had to be extremely brief. How brief? One of the polonium isotopes studied by Gentry has a half-life of three minutes! Another has a half-life of only 164 microseconds!

In the evolutionary model, the time required for the cooling and solidification of these granites is millions and millions of years. Gentry believes these halos to constitute powerful evidence against evolution and its presumed vast time spans. He believes these halos speak of a very rapid formation of these crustal rocks. To quote Gentry:

> ...unless the creation of the radioactivity and rocks were simultaneous there would be no ... pleochroic halos. ... the radioactivity and formation of the rocks must be almost instantaneous.
>
> Could the earth have been created by fiat? ... no one has thus far proposed an alternative concept that will account for the variant halos" [pp. 78–79].[5]

5. Robert V. Gentry, "Cosmology and earth's invisible realm," *Medical Opinion and Review,* October 1967, p. 65ff.

12

Time: Evolution's Friend or Foe?

For a thousand years in thy sight are but as yesterday
when it is past, and as a watch in the night.   Ps. 90:4

The argument of this book is that the universe is quite
young. If the universe can be shown to be young, then
evolution is ruled out, since all agree that the evolutionary
process requires vast numbers of years. Time is often viewed
as the great friend of evolution, supposedly performing all
the miracles of creation that in the Bible are attributed to
God. The famous Harvard professor George Wald has explained
the evolutionists' view of the importance of time as follows:

> The important point is that since the origin of life belongs
> in the category of at-least-once phenomena, time is on its
> side. However improbable we regard this event . . . given
> enough time it will almost certainly happen at least
> once. . . . Time is in fact the hero of the plot. . . . Given so
> much time, the "impossible" becomes possible, the possible
> probable, and the probable virtually certain. One has only to
> wait; time itself performs miracles. [1]

Of Monkeys and Typewriters

A better-known form of the evolution-through-limitless-
time argument is the monkey-and-typewriter illustration.
Physicist William R. Bennett, Jr., has stated it this way:
"Nearly everyone knows that if enough monkeys were al-
lowed to pound away at typewriters for enough time, all the
great works of literature would result."[2]
Something about this argument is intuitively persuasive.

1. George Wald, "The Origin of Life," in *The Physics and Chemistry of Life*, by the
editors of *Scientific American* (New York: Simon and Schuster, 1955): 12.
2. W. R. Bennett, Jr., "How Artificial Is Intelligence?" *American Scientist* 65
(November-December 1977): 694.

Obviously, if the monkeys were to type long enough, one of them would inevitably type the word *to,* and with just a little more time surely no one would be surprised to find the word *two.* And if such circumstances produced *to* and *two,* then why not eventually *four, eight,* and finally a complete sentence, paragraph, and so on?

The question of whether or not time is actually on the side of evolution, as Wald and Bennett maintain, is an important one even if, as this book argues, there is very little of it to work with. The fact of the matter is that time is not a friend of evolution. It is evolution's enemy.

To put it simply, if a monkey is going to type a literary work, it will need to get the job done in a hurry. Time will work against the monkey's literary efforts as well as against any similar uphill evolutionary process in the real world. This fact is reflected in what scientists call the Second Law of Thermodynamics, which states that all real processes in the physical universe—when isolated and left to themselves—go irreversibly downhill toward increasing disorder and chaos.

In terms of the typewriting-monkey example, it means that along with the accumulating chance of producing something meaningful as time increases, there must also be a consideration of the more rapidly accumulating chance that the monkey, typewriter, or both will break down. Thus, the longer the monkey types, the greater the chance that its typewriter will break. If it would take a million years for the monkey to accidentally hammer out something as meaningful as a good poem or short story, there is no chance whatsoever that the typewriter would last that long—to mention nothing of the monkey or its paper supply! Evolution only works in the imaginations of evolutionist scholars like George Wald and William R. Bennett. In the real world, any system posited to produce ordered and meaningful outcomes will inevitably be subject to the processes of decay and disordering known to scientists as the law of entropy (Second Law of Thermodynamics). Time is no friend of evolution.

Time Rushes On

The flight of time's arrow is downward rather than upward, as evolutionists claim. Its passage tends to work against evolution instead of for it, and in this sense it is evolution's foe. But there is another sense in which time works against evolution, and realization of it flows from the same stream of scientific data that indicates a recent creation. The discoveries that point to a recent creation also indicate that deterioration processes are occurring at a rate that is unfathomable for any evolutionist. The same sort of evidence that indicates, for example, that the sun has not been burning for a million years into the past also indicates that it cannot continue to burn for a million years into the future. As we lose the distant recesses of the past, it seems we are also losing the distant future as well.

The explosion in scientific technology in space and earth exploration is enabling a degree of detailed and continuous data monitoring unheard of only a few years ago. On the basis of what we now know, creationists can predict that this continuous monitoring will begin showing more and more evidences of rapid decay. Many new clocks will turn up, and many present creationist clocks should prove verifiable by direct tests and measurements. If the thesis of this book is correct, the proper word to the wise is not only that "time is short" but also that "it is later than you think."

What If Scientists Disprove the Bible?

With all that has been shown, many Christians continue to worry about the possibility that someone is going to make a discovery that will disprove the Bible. Those who are troubled by such fears must begin to grasp an understanding of the limitations of science and what it can and cannot do. With the wisdom of hindsight provided by several hundred years of scientific endeavor, we can say with confidence that almost every day some non-believing scientist *will* come up with "evidence" that purportedly disproves the Bible. This has been going on for centuries.

But what has also become clear is that God is always raising up believing scholars and scientists to make new discoveries in support of the Bible as well as to figure out why the old "proofs" against its testimony were not really proofs after all. In the end one realizes that faith in God and his Word is not primarily an intellectual issue but a spiritual one.

Scientific arguments against the Bible come and go. Some are rather easily dismissed, while others hold sway for a good long while. Eventually, however, new evidence or new insight will reveal that the Bible stands as the ultimate truth. This book is simply an account of the latest chapter in the never-ending story of God's ability to defend his Holy Scriptures against the assaults of proud and arrogant unbelievers. And so it will ever be. "The grass withereth, the flower fadeth: but the word of our God shall stand for ever" (Isa. 40:8).

13

Yesterday, Today, and Forever

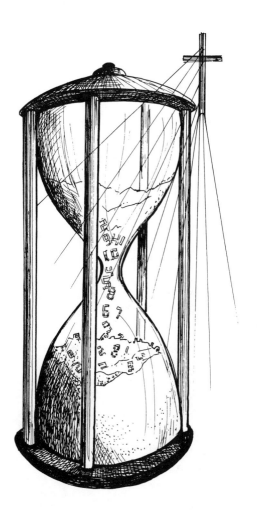

Jesus Christ the same yesterday, and to day, and for ever.   *Heb.* 13:8

At the beginning of this book a question from the Bible was posed for the reader: "Am I a God at hand . . . and not a God afar off?" (Jer. 23:23). In the sense of scientific evidences for when he created all things, this book has shown that God is very close to us indeed. Scientists have been saying for many years that God's creation was very far away in time, but now the evidence is showing us that this is not the case.

It is the same in our personal lives. God so often seems far away, but as he bears witness through nature that the time of his creation of all things is quite recent, so he bears witness through the Bible that he is personally near. God created the beautiful world around us a few thousand years ago. He also created us in his image for the purpose of close fellowship in loving obedience. But we disobeyed our loving Creator, and, as he had warned, death, sin, suffering, and separation from his fellowship entered into the perfect world God had created. Through our sin, we brought death and decay not only upon ourselves but on the rest of creation as well. The world and all that is in it became cursed for our sake, and so it remains to this day (Rom. 8:22).

But the story does not end there. The loving God who created us made provision that we might return to close fellowship and eternal life with him. He—God the Son— became one of us, lived a perfect life without sin, and then died on the cross for our sin. To prove that he was God and had gained victory over sin and death, he arose from the grave after three days. The Scripture says that if we proclaim with our lips that Jesus Christ is our Lord and believe in our hearts that God did raise him from the dead, we will be saved and enter into eternal life (Rom. 10:9).

In a discussion with his disciples, Jesus once said that on the basis of their close personal and spiritual knowledge of him, they should believe in his divine nature and mission—

but if they could not believe on that basis, they should believe in him on the basis of the miracles and works they had seen him perform (John 14:9–11). In the same manner, he honored the honest skepticism of his disciple Thomas, who said, "Except I shall see in his hands the print of the nails, and put my finger into the print of the nails, and thrust my hand into his side, I will not believe" (John 20:25). The resurrected Jesus later appeared to Thomas and lovingly answered his doubts by saying to him, "Reach hither thy finger, and behold my hands; and reach hither thy hand, and thrust it into my side: and be not faithless, but believing" (v. 27). When Thomas was confronted by the evidence, he spoke to Jesus with the immortal words, "My Lord and my God" (v. 28).

Believe in God. Believe in his Son, Jesus Christ. And believe in his holy and eternal Word, the Bible. Believe for the sake of the spiritual knowledge you have of God through faith. Or else believe on the basis of his many wonderful works, such as the evidences in this book that point to "his eternal power and Godhead" (Rom. 1:20). The point is—be not faithless, but believing.

Appendix
Scripture Evidence For a Young World

The following points are a summary of the biblical doctrine of a young creation:

1. God spoke the following words directly to Moses: "For in six days the LORD made the heavens and the earth, the sea and all that is in them..." (Exod. 20:11, NASB).

2. Genesis 1 specifically says that each of the six days of creation consisted of one evening and one morning. For example: "And there was evening and there was morning, a fifth day" (Gen. 1:23, NASB).

3. Adam and Eve were created on the sixth day (Gen. 1:27; cf. Gen. 2) and became the parents of all the people that have ever lived (Gen. 3:20). Genesis 5:5 states that Adam lived 930 years before he died. Therefore, the time from the sixth day of creation until Adam's death was 930 years. We know the creation days were short in duration because (1) they each consisted of one morning and evening, and (2) Adam lived through at least part of the sixth day plus the entire seventh day and still lived "only" 930 years.

4. Genesis 5 and 11 provide a detailed genealogy from Adam to Abraham. Gaps are precluded because the age of each patriarch is given at the age of his son's birth. We are told, for example, that "Seth lived one hundred and five years, and became the father of Enosh" (Gen. 5:6, NASB). We are also told how old each patriarch was at his death.

121

Thus, the time frame from creation to Abraham is clearly on the order of a few thousand years.

5. The historical lineage from Abraham to the present is well understood. Scripture provides a detailed history from Abraham to Christ, and our present calendar measures from Christ to the present. The total time period is again a matter of a few thousand years.

6. What about the time-gap theory? Lucifer was the chief of God's created angels and rebelled against God and fell from his original state of beauty and perfection. We now know him as Satan or the devil. Some have suggested that Lucifer's fall occurred before the six creation days, during a time gap between Genesis 1:1 and 1:2.

The theory of a gap between Genesis 1:1 and 1:2 (during which Lucifer was created and fell) cannot be true, because Ezekiel 28:13 tells us that Lucifer in his pre-fall state of splendor and beauty was in the Garden of Eden. Scripture also states clearly that Eden was planted during the six creation days (Gen. 2:4–9), and therefore Lucifer's fall cannot have been prior to the six days of creation.

We also know that on Day Six, God saw all that he had made and it was still "very good" (Gen. 1:31). Exodus 20:11 confirms that God created all that is in heaven and earth in six days. Lucifer/Satan is in heaven and earth. Therefore, he cannot have preceded the six creation days, and his fall cannot have been before Day Six.

Bibliography

Akridge, Russell. "The Sun Is Shrinking," *Impact*, No. 82, April 1980 (Institute for Creation Research, 2716 Madison Ave., San Diego, CA 92116).

Awbrey, Frank T. "Space Dust, the Moon's Surface, and the Age of the Cosmos," *Creation/Evolution*, Issue XIII, pp. 21–29.

Bahcall, John N. and Davis, Raymond, Jr. "Solar Neutrinos: A Scientific Puzzle," *Science* 191 (1976): 264–267.

Bennett, W. R., Jr. "How Artificial Is Intelligence?" *American Scientist* 65 (November-December 1977); 694–702.

Dillow, Jody. "The Catastrophic Deep-Freeze of the Beresovka Mammoth," *Creation Research Society Quarterly* 14 (June 1977): 5–12.

Dixon, Robert T. *Dynamic Astronomy* (Englewood Cliffs, NJ: Prentice Hall, Inc., 1971).

Dunham, David W.; Sofia, Sabatino; Fiala, Alan D.; Herald, David W. and Muller, Paul M. "Observations of a Probable Change in the Solar Radius Between 1715 and 1979," *Science* 210 (12 December 1980): 1243–1245.

"Dust Rings Our Solar System," *Wichita Eagle and Beacon*, 10 November 1983, p. 1A ff.

Eddy, John A. and Boornazian, Aram A. "Analyses of Historical Data Suggest Sun Is Shrinking," *Physics Today* 32, No. 9 (September 1979): 17.

"Eyes on Jupiter," *Life* (May 1979), pp. 44–47.

Funkhouser, John G. and Naughton, John J. "Radiogenic Helium and Argon in Ultramafic Inclusions from Hawaii," *Journal for Geophysical Research* 73, No. 14 (15 July 1968): 4601–4607.

Gentry, Robert V. "Cosmology and Earth's Invisible Realm," *Medical Opinion and Review,* October 1967, p. 65ff.

Gentry, Robert V., et al. "Radiohalos in Coalified Wood: New Evidence Relating to the Time of Uranium Introduction and Coalification," *Science* 194 (15 October 1976): 315–317.

Hawkings, G. S. (ed.). *Meteor Orbits and Dust, Smithsonian Contributions Astrophysics,* vol. 2 (Washington, D.C: Smithsonian Institution and NASA, 1976).

Kazmann, Raphael G. "It's About Time: 4.5 Billion Years," *Geotimes,* September 1978, pp. 18–20.

Morris, Henry. *The Remarkable Birth of Planet Earth.* (San Diego, CA: Creation-Life Pub., 1973).

Morton, Glenn R.; Slusher, Harold S.; and Mandock, Richard E. "The Age of Lunar Craters," *Creation Research Society Quarterly* 20 (September 1983): 105–108.

Parkinson, John H.; Morrison, Leslie V.; and Stephenson, F. Richard. "The Constancy of the Solar Diameter Over the Past 250 Years," *Nature* 288 (11 December 1980): 548–551.

Parkinson, John H. "New Measurements of the Solar Diameter," *Nature* 304 (11 August 1983): 518–520.

Setterfield, Barry. "An Asteroid Tilts the Earth?" *Ex Nihilo,* April 1983, pp. 6–8.

Shapiro, Irwin I. "Is the Sun Shrinking?" *Science* 208 (4 April 1980): 51–53.

Shore, Steven N. "Footprints in the Dust: The Lunar Surface and Creationism," *Creation/Evolution,* Issue XIV, p 32–35.

Slusher, Harold S. "A Young Universe," *Bible-Science Newsletter* 13 (January 1975): 1ff.

Slusher, Harold S. *Age of the Cosmos: ICR Technical Monograph #9* (San Diego: Institute for Creation Research [2716 Madison Ave., San Diego, CA 92116], 1980).

Smith, Robert F. "Origins and Civil Liberties." *Creation Social Science and Humanities Quarterly,* 3 (Winter 1980): 23–27.

Stevenson, P. "Meteoritic Evidence for a Young Earth," *Creation Research Society Quarterly* 12 (June 1975): 23.

"The Faint Young Sun and the Warm Earth," *Science News* 111 (5 March 1977): 154.

"The Fingerprints of God: Interview With Robert V. Gentry," *Ministry,* November 1981, pp. 20–21.

The Rand McNally New Concise Atlas of the Universe (London: Mitchell Beazley Pub. Ltd. [87–89 Shaftesbury Ave., London W1V 7AD], 1978).

"The Sun Is Shrinking," *Wichita Eagle and Beacon,* 23 March 1980, p. 6B.

Wald, George. "The Origin of Life." *The Physics and Chemistry of Life,* by the editors of *Scientific American* (New York: Simon and Schuster, 1955): 3–26.

Wieland, Carl. "An Asteroid Tilts the Earth," *Ex Nihilo,* January 1983, pp. 12–14.

"Workers Find Whale in Diatomaceous Earth Quarry," *Chemical and Engineering News,* 11 October 1976, p. 40.

Wysong, R. L. *The Creation-Evolution Controversy* (Midland, MI: Inquiry Press, 1976).

Index